ARRIVING WHERE I STARTED

1931 – 1961: A MEMOIR

MAGGIE SMITH

Published in 2015 by FeedARead.com Publishing

Copyright © Maggie Smith

First Edition

A CIP catalogue record for this title is available from the British
Library.

Also by Maggie Smith

Branching Out: A Workbook for Early Retirement
The Best Is Yet to Come: A Workbook for the Middle Years
Changing Course: A Positive Approach to a New Job or Lifestyle
Journeys in the Bookshop (Editor) Woolfson & Tay
A Handbook for U3A Creative Writing Groups
Glimpses Through the Curtains
Associating in the Turbine Hall

Arriving Where I Started

We shall not cease from exploration
And the end of all our exploring
Will be to arrive where we started
And know the place for the first time.
                    Four Quartets - T S Eliot

INSTRUMENTS AND OTHER MYSTERIES

I must have been about four when I heard my mother tell someone she'd had instruments when I was born. So where were they? Our house was small, I'd know if there were drums or a piano anywhere. Or even a trumpet. The tale was repeated and I finally dared ask

'What sort of instruments did you have, Mummy?'

Asking questions might be cheeky; cheek was not encouraged.

'What *are* you talking about, silly?'

I was so used to being called 'Silly' it was like a nickname.

'When I was born? You told Auntie…'

Mum laughed. I was used to that too.

'You'll understand when you're older.'

So much had to wait until I was older. I never did get to understand all of it.

'Not putting on weight was your worst problem.'

I knew about the weight, everyone we met heard how I'd failed to thrive for my first few months. I wasn't sure if thriving was like walking.

'Lucky it was a hot summer,' Mum said one day on the way home from tea with Uncle Charlie and Aunt Rose, 'You were out in the sun all day. it was vitamins that kept you alive. Never knew you were there, you never cried, not even when the dog jumped on your pram and growled. You were too weak to cry.'

What were vitamins? I didn't know why she was telling me, but she and Aunt Rose had been talking for ages about how I couldn't digest milk and had ended up with a mixture of cows' milk and barley water. That sounded disgusting and was probably why I hated milk. Still, Mum sounded pleased that I didn't cry. I decided I would try never to cry.

Conversations like this with Mum usually ended with

'Go and play. It'll soon be time for dinner – tea – your bedtime cocoa.'

My day was punctuated with reminders of the next meal. Going to play meant either to my bedroom, where my toys were kept so I didn't untidy the downstairs rooms, or into the garden, mostly alone or with imaginary friends. I had no brothers or sisters and having anyone over to play made Mum grumble

'I don't have time to keep polishing the floors.'

There would be pursed lips and anxious hovering in case a crumb or a droplet of lemonade was spilt.

Playing in the garden was more fun. Iris English from next-door-but-one was allowed to come over as long as we didn't tread mud indoors. We would hold dolls' tea parties until Iris told her Mum, who told mine, that I ate the dirt which was our pretend cake. Neither mother ever thought to give us real cake. I ate coal, too and peeled wallpaper from the sitting room wall, undiscovered for weeks as I squatted behind the sofa. Mum cleaned all the time, so I don't know why it took so long to find the scraps of paper. Perhaps she only cleaned where people would see.

Every night I knelt by my bed to say my prayers:
'God bless Daddy and Mum and Gran and make me a good girl. For Jews Crysay came in.'
Who this Jews Crysay was, or why and where he or she came in was like many grown-up sayings, puzzling, until I could read a prayer book at Sunday School and learned it was
'For Jesus Christ's sake. Amen.'
Prayer obviously didn't work. I was always in trouble, rarely the good girl I'd asked God to make me into. Sunday school teachers said God always answered prayers if only to say 'No,' so there didn't seem much point in asking.

The Gran I asked God to bless was Mum's mother. I had only Gran and one Granddad. Dad's mother died from breast cancer before he and Mum had met. Granddads were the opposite – Mum's father died when she was 19, he killed himself. I didn't know people did that and she didn't talk about it much. I knew Dad's father, but not very well as Dad didn't like him, said he was a drunk. Grandpa rarely came to see us but I do remember a damp white moustache which smelt awful when he kissed me. Gran often looked after me while Mum was at work. Most people's mothers stayed home to look after the house and children, but mine worked in London, as manageress of a shop called Marks and Spencer Penny Bazaar.

Gran was very old, she had seen Queen Victoria and when I was three we had a special birthday tea for Gran's 70th birthday. She was often cross, I was always being told
'Don't do that' or 'Wait till your mother comes home.'
She would take me shopping in Welling High Street and I would dawdle behind. It was always the same shops; the baker for Gran's

doughnuts, plus one for me, then into a shop called an Off Licence. Gran loved her stout, not made of fat but in a bottle. She must occasionally have removed her hat, but for me her head was permanently covered by this large brown object, a bit like a trilby but minus the dent.

Gran in her best hat

I wondered if she kept it on in bed and wondered too if she might be a witch. Gran always wore an overall, crossed over at the front like a dress, even when we went out. She had big boots too, laced at the front. I used to help her pull them off, either because they were truly stuck or because it was a game, which was unlikely, as she didn't seem to like children. If she met neighbours at the shops she would recite lurid tales of my crimes.

Not emptying my plate was a major sin. Gran would complain to me 'I cooked for lords and ladies who were far more grateful than you.' Gran and her two sisters, my Great-Aunts, had been housekeepers and maids to the gentry, whoever they were. My mouth always watered over her steamed apple or rhubarb suet puddings and most of all when it was Dad's favourite, steak and kidney, so I don't know why I didn't empty my plate for Gran. Except that she also cooked bacon pudding with a foul black herb that caught between the teeth and served Camp coffee with the milk on the turn, which meant floating specks you were supposed to ignore. I shudder at the memory of grilled herrings with bones in. I hear Gran's 'Bury them in the mashed potato and you won't notice.'
She was wrong and the only fish bones I can bear are those in tinned salmon, the ones that look like teeth. Neither oxtail nor Irish stew, more bones you were not supposed to notice, have ever appeared in my kitchen. She piled the plates so high too, I nearly always ate everything Mum gave me.

3

I was always naughty, including the day I poked a feather duster through the spokes of the fireguard and ran round the room brandishing the foul-smelling results. Then there was the time I fell in the paddling pool in Danson Park, soaking my clothes and in deep trouble, even though a bigger boy had accidentally tripped me. Out came the regular
 'Just wait till your mother gets home,'
but Mum never punished me, except to make sure I said sorry when it was necessary. Sometimes she looked as if she wanted to laugh. Life was very confusing.

One day Gran had promised me a treat if we heard the 'Stop Me and Buy One' chant from the man on the funny bicycle with the box on the front. My favourite was the 'lolly tube,' with a stick at each end to hold as we turned the frozen juice around to lick, chins scarlet or blue with melted dribbles. Gran gave me a penny from her apron pocket, but by the time I got to the front gate the bike was almost round the corner. A bigger boy who lived across the road beckoned me to follow him. Together we turned the corner, ran along the street and round the next corner. The 'Stop Me and Buy One' man had pulled up a few yards ahead. I looked round, had no idea where I was, panicked and turned back. Gran was standing at our corner, witch's hat firmly on her head, arms folded across her apron. I knew what came next.
'Wait till your mother gets home, Miss.'
Mum was kinder.
'And you didn't get your ice cream. Never mind.'

Perhaps the very worst time was the syrup of figs episode. It was for me. I didn't hate all medicines; Cod Liver Oil and Malt 'to put some flesh on those bones;' (definitely worked) would have me salivating, though I did conquer my addiction to Californian Syrup of Figs. An empty kitchen, Gran upstairs, Mum at work, a chair nearby to reach the top shelf of the cupboard where bottles were kept out of the reach of small fingers. Syrup of Figs poured liberally down both throat and jumper. Mum actually laughed.
'She'll get her come-uppance'
was her response to Gran's tale-telling. How true; a miserable day spent mostly in the bathroom.
More serious episodes included stealing, but the threat of prison acted as a lifetime deterrent. Mum would sometimes take me shopping on Saturdays and I learned to shoplift as we walked past

4

Woolworth's sweet counters piled with cascades of bonbons. There were more kinds of sweets, but it was bonbons I craved, in white wrappers with pictures of luscious fruits. I wasn't allowed to eat them very often, as

'They'll rot your teeth.'

I loved the crunch as I cracked them to find the chewy centres. A few dangling over the edge of the display slid easily into my coat pocket. The shop could spare them and no-one would notice.

Except Mum. She'd warned me she had eyes in the back of her head; I never saw them, but was absolutely convinced they were hidden under her hair.

'Margaret.' I was definitely in trouble. 'I saw what you put in your pocket. It's stealing. I must tell the manager. If he calls the police you might go to prison.'

She marched me down an endless corridor, grasping my hand hard so I couldn't run away. Where would I run? She stood still and I nearly tripped over her feet.

'I think he's gone for dinner, you're a lucky girl. Give me the sweets.'

We returned to the counter, Mum handed back the bonbons and I muttered an apology to the assistant. I was sent to bed early, never questioning how Mum knew the manager was at lunch. Or had she decided I'd learned my lesson and the manager might laugh?

Anyone unwary enough to ask my name was surprised by:

'Margate-In-The-Rain-Fairman-203-Elsa-Road-Welling-Kent.'

My name was Margaret Lorraine Fairman. I never left the house without an adult, but once I could walk and talk Mum took care to ensure there was no risk that I would get lost. Welling was a nondescript between–the-wars dormitory suburb, Elsa Road part of an estate with identical semi-detached two-down-three-up houses, plus kitchen and a bathroom with a gas geyser, which popped alarmingly when the pilot light was ignited for my bath.

Keith Wagstaff was my playmate, a year or so younger than me, the baby in a large family next door. Uncle Jim, who was a milkman and home in the afternoons would bring Keith over to play. Dad and Uncle Jim would drink tea or sometimes stuff from bottles while

Keith Wagstaff and me

they talked about Auntie Mabel. I hadn't seen her for some time, she wasn't well and Keith was only just three when she died. I wasn't quite sure what 'died' was but Uncle Jim stopped smiling and soon they all moved away. That summer Dad looked after me all day, because he was out of work. I didn't know what that meant, he did the sort of work Mum did in the house and he let me help him dry the dishes. I would hear loud arguments between Mum and Dad, words like
'It's not my fault there's a Depression,'
but he never seemed to be home for long.

We once had a greengrocers' shop, with our hall and front room full of boxes of fruit and vegetables I was warned never to touch. Another time I saw him in a white overall at the local Co-op. The box of tin checks collected from there helped me learn my sums as I played shops on our blue embossed carpet. The colour and pattern were written on my heart after they were both so angry the day I spilt ink on it and the stain never quite came out.

Dad was often cross, but he would sometimes let me play with his hair before I went to bed, poking about with Mum's metal curlers until he'd had enough. I would hear him go straight to the bathroom, I think he wanted to rinse out the curls and Brylcreem his hair so it was smooth again. He spent hours in the garage tinkering with his motor cycle and sidecar, which I loved riding in. Mum always told me he was disappointed that I wasn't a boy, but that summer he taught me to ride a bike, gripping the back of the saddle as I steered the bike down the path towards the garage. One day I charged into the garage door, waiting for

'Brake, clumsy!'
Instead, there was applause. He'd let go of the saddle. I was riding by myself!

One evening I woke, scared possibly by a dream. I went to find a grownup and discovered the house was empty. It was still broad daylight, the coverlet on my parents' bed pulled smoothly over the pillows. Downstairs I tore through the house. Not difficult, front sitting room, rarely used except when we had visitors, small dining room, table set for supper for two and the kitchen. An older child might have noticed that the back door was ajar, but by then I was a hysterical four-year-old. Abandoned, orphaned, done for, my parents gone for ever. Inconsolable, I went back to their bedroom. A soggy heap curled on the coverlet, I heard Mum asking 'Whatever's the matter?'
as she picked me up and cuddled me, shushing my sobs. She'd been talking across the garden fences to Auntie Glad. Dad would have been on his way home from work, they had not had supper. I'd been in bed only half an hour or so.

In summer 1935, I went to my first 'royal' event, King George V's Silver Jubilee. Mum and Dad, Uncle Ernie and Auntie Doll took me to what they called a ceremony in Danson Park. Uncle Ernie was Dad's brother and he'd just married Auntie Doll, who worked for Mum. I had new clothes in Union Jack colours, a blue pleated skirt, white blouse, a red, white and blue ribbon in my hair and a jubilee medal with red, white and blue ribbons pinned to my chest.

Silver Jubilee in Danson Park with Mum

Iris lived next door to the Wagstaffs with her parents, Mum's friend Auntie Glad who looked after me sometimes and Mr English, who was never an Uncle anybody, or not to me. I still hear his irritable

7

'For God's sake can't you kids shut up?'
when the football results were broadcast on a Saturday night.
Auntie Glad explained.
'He wants to check his Pools.'
I was never sure how he managed without getting wet. No-one in
our house went near pools. Except the time I fell into the one in
Danson Park.

At Elsa Road I was made to finish my dinner even if I had a sore
throat. Once a cross doctor came in the night and jammed a spoon
down that aching throat. Doctors worked at night and on Saturdays
too, so I expect she was tired. Calling a doctor to the house was
unusual, it meant someone had to go to a public phone box. Then
they had to pay for the visit, the 'Panel' we belonged to covered
only my Dad's health and that only when he was in work. They may
also have paid into some kind of Hospital Saturday Fund. My
constant visits to Great Ormond Street Children's Hospital until my
tonsils were removed when I was six would have made this
essential. I can still smell and taste my horrible medicines: Fennon's
Fever Curer; Vicks Vapour rub burning my chest, Gran's home-
made cure-all, onions steeped in vinegar and sugar. Most of them
were horrible.

My aunts' and uncles' names were confusing. Dad's oldest sister
Rose married a Charlie Rabbitt and Mum's brother Charles married
a tiny Irishwoman, also named Rose. We called them by different
names which made it easier. Dad's lot, my favourites, were Aunt
Rose and Uncle Charlie; Mum's brother was Uncle Charles, his wife
Auntie Rosie. Their son, my cousin Philip, was eight years older
than me. I often spent days at their house, I suppose the thirties
equivalent of child-minding.

Philip used to tease me all the time. One day he played a dreadful
trick on me when Auntie Rosie had gone shopping.
'Philip, you're old enough to take care of your cousin,'
she told him before she went. I was playing in the garden. Later I
came indoors, wiping my shoes properly and trotting upstairs, in a
hurry but not quite desperate.
As I sat on the toilet a deep growl came from outside the bathroom
window
'I am the fiend of the toilet. I eat little girls for supper if they cry.'
Cry? Sobbing, I pulled up my knickers before I'd finished. It couldn't
really be a fiend, could it? Fumbling at the door I forgot I'd put the

bolt on. The growl again.

'Ho, ho, ho, I told you not to cry, little girl. Cry-babies get punished.'

I thought someone was climbing in the window, though the gap was too small to admit a human. Knickers corkscrewed round my legs, I saw floating through the window a twist of screwed-up newspaper, smoke coming from its tail like a burning aeroplane, flames dying as it curled onto the lino.

'Put it out, stamp on it or you'll be in trouble. I can see your bum. Silly girl. Open the door and shut up bawling, it's only a bit of fun.'

Did Philip really think burning me to death was fun? The smell of the charred paper made my nose and eyes run. I suddenly remembered the bolt and opened the door. Philip pushed past me, dustpan in hand, shouting something about burn marks on the floor. What would Auntie Rosie say? I might not be allowed to come again. I wouldn't mind, if it meant not being left with Philip, but there were always cream cakes for tea. I was afraid of my cousin. He grew out of his teasing and we became better friends, but never close ones.

THE NEXT STEP

Not yet five, I'm off for a great adventure. It's my first day at school, Brampton Road Junior Mixed and Infants. I'm gripping Mum's hand very hard while Auntie Glad holds my other hand and Iris trots ahead to join her friends. She's seven, nearly a junior and used to first days of term. We go through huge gates and I tread carefully over an asphalt playground heaving with barbarian hordes, cowering near Mum's coat among the other new infants. The hordes part, suddenly quiet, to make way for a grey-haired giant; it's the Headmaster, Mr Thomas. His voice is clear but I'm so scared I don't hear a word he says. I know for certain only that I must be good and am equally certain that this is beyond me. I am constantly in trouble over unexplained misdemeanours, some even more serious than the feather duster. Mothers wave to us and disappear. I am herded into a room filled with rows of small chairs in pairs at equally small tables, like my own small blue chair Father Christmas brought me. This must be the 'class' Mum told me I'd be in, with a teacher so I can learn to write and read books. I can already do both, so why do I have to come here?

First school photo

Soon after I start school it's my birthday. My special treat is a visit to the cinema, wherever that is. Dad says it will be glamorous; I'm not sure what that means, but I adore Jessie Matthews, the singing and high-kicking star. I can read the title, 'Highway', it's not really a film for children but I know I will remember until I'm a very old lady the rows of seats in the dark, the lights going on suddenly, Dad buying me an ice cream. Then walking home in my new wellington boots and splashing in puddles made mysterious with lamp-lit shadows, Mum and Dad holding my hands, letting me jump and even squeal without once 'Shushing' me.

After the first week at school I walk there alone, meeting friends on the way. In this quiet neighbourhood cars are rare and we often pass a policeman. I've been allowed out without a grown-up for some time and I know I must never speak to strange men. One day we are with Brian, who is a show-off. He trips as he hops on and off the pavement and is run over by a bike. A policeman soon arrives to wrap a handkerchief round his bloodied knee, and to tell him off both for
'Making such a row with all that wailing,'
and for making the cyclist fall off his bike. After that we still jump over cracks in paving stones but don't dare step in the gutter. Brian isn't badly hurt; the cross policeman has done him good and he behaves himself.

Those of us who could read before we went to school were made 'monitors' and given tasks like getting new chalks from the stock cupboard. Every morning before the first lesson we would sit with other children who couldn't yet read and listen as they practised aloud. Handwriting was a different matter and I never managed to write legibly, but at least I was never forced to use my right hand, a fairly progressive move in 1936.

A very sad thing happened towards the end of the school year. My friend Joy Fletcher was invited to tea one Monday, but at school assembly we were told Joy had died in an accident and was never coming back. We said a special prayer and had to ask our Mummies for some money towards something called a wreath. Our teacher was crying when she said
'Joy ran into the road and was hit by a car. Please be very careful on your way home.'
I was quite excited by having news to break, but puzzled by
'Never coming back.'
We'd buried a bird the cat had killed. I knew that my Grandpa and one of my Grandmas had gone to heaven before I was born, but grandparents are old. Joy was only a child, like me.

I told Mum Joy wasn't coming to tea because she was dead. Horrified, she said
'That's a wicked thing to say. It's straight to bed with no tea for you. Did you and Joy fall out? You know you must never tell lies, especially such dreadful ones.'
There was no way I could convince her. Phones, TV and local radio stations were rarities and most parents did not congregate at the school gates so there was no immediate grapevine. Later in the evening Auntie Glad dropped in to tell Mum the awful news. Iris was older and had told the story more convincingly. Mum said she was sorry, but I was upset that she hadn't believed me. Joy had been shopping on Saturday with her older sister Audrey, ran away from her into the road and was killed outright.
I was on an errand and must have been between classrooms when Joy's wreath was sent round for us all to see, so I was unlucky. It was in the shape of the school badge, grey and blue, in as near a match of plants and flowers as they could find. I always minded not knowing what Joy's wreath looked like. Perhaps even a small child needs tangible evidence of 'never coming back.' My mother didn't know Joy's parents and never mentioned her name again, yet almost eighty years later I recall nearly every detail and wonder how the family and especially Audrey coped.

Dad didn't like holidays but Mum and Auntie Glad would take Iris and me away. One year we went to Sunshine Holiday Camp where we were runners-up in a fancy dress competition .

Second prize!

My first kiss took place at Brampton Road. Alan Fisher sat in front of me and his damply giggling attempt landed somewhere below my ear. The boy who sat next to him told me later that Alan had been dared to kiss the first girl he saw in class that day. Not exactly the romance of my life, but it was a start!

A few months after I started school we'd moved a few streets away to a new housing estate. Our address was now Bexleyheath, slightly more desirable than Welling. It may have been the first house anyone in our families had owned, or would be once the thing called a mortgage was paid. The land had previously been an orchard so we had three apple trees in the garden. As it was on a corner, 116 Gipsy Road cost £50 more than neighbouring houses for the privilege of a fenced garden. Without the slightest idea what it meant, I overheard Mum saying the corner made us 'a cut above the neighbours.'
For £400 my father (women rarely owned property) became a householder. Difficult to imagine such prices, but his weekly wage was probably around £4. On Friday evenings I would often watch him give Mum some money from a brown envelope.

The kitchen at the new house was always spotlessly clean, with a floor you could certainly eat off, though any attempt to do so would be met with disgust. I suspect Mum, if not Dad, yearned for middle class respectability. Her kitchen outfit always included an apron and rubber gloves. She was obsessively hygienic, yet on liver and bacon day she coated the liver with flour sprinkled onto a newspaper, (to keep the worktop clean, she said), a cigarette drooping from her lips. I waited every time for the ash to drop onto the meat, but she always seemed to focus at crisis point and tap the ash into the sink. I can still summon the smell of the disinfectant poured down the sink after every washing up, the casement window open in the coldest weather to dispel any hint of cooking. Even the delicious and rare aroma of cake baking was banished, but I was allowed to stir the mix and eat any remains from the bowl, a still favourite ritual for any child. Our diet was highly predictable – Sunday roast, Monday cold meat with bubble and squeak, Tuesday shepherd's pie, probably sausages or liver next, then Friday was fish, though we were not Catholics. I don't think we went to church, though I was sent to Sunday school.

The new kitchen cabinet was Mum's proof of status. The suburban version of a Welsh dresser, the lower section had a cupboard and drawers, but it was the top half which fascinated me with its pull-down enamel worktop, white with dark blue edging which, to Mum's chagrin, was soon chipped in places. Once the cupboard was opened treasures were revealed, a flour mill where I was allowed to turn the handle, until the day I forgot to put a bowl underneath to catch the sifted flour. Punishment was swift but never physical, I would usually be sent to spend the next hour or so in my bedroom. Weeks elapsed before I was allowed to go near the shelf again, even to lift an egg from the fitted rack. Other shelves held tins of rice, sultanas and the dreaded tapioca, known among my friends, but never in front of Mum, as frogspawn.

Respectability was so vital that not only the washing-up but the drying-up must be completed after every meal. Anyone passing the fence might peer over, notice clean but undried crockery on the draining board and condemn my mother's slovenly habits. Cleanliness was not only next to godliness, it was way ahead, but there may have been reasons. It was possibly a compulsion influenced by the trauma of her discovery at nineteen, when she came home from work one evening, of her father's body.

It is one of the few stories from her early life she told me. He had killed himself by drinking ammonia and from the shock of this terrible event she had a complete breakdown and was in hospital for some time. She adored her dad but not her mother and she blamed Gran for Grandad's suicide. I can hear Mum saying
'My dad couldn't find work. He'd been a caretaker and got the sack so they had to leave their home. She used to nag him non-stop and he'd had enough. Her darling Charlie was married so she'd lost his rent and I don't think she liked me much.'
It was like listening to a gruesome Brothers Grimm tale. I was quite scared and didn't really want to know. The other stories? I knew that her brother Charles, who was five years older, always bullied her. She could remember going to school perched on his skate while he said things like
'We were all right before you came. Why don't you just clear off?'
Girls always seemed to be less important than boys, even in Mum's day and she said he might have liked her more if she'd been a brother. The other story I remember was a kind of morality tale.
'My mother asked if I'd been at the condensed milk tin and I said "No," but it was dripping all down my jumper. I got beaten with her slipper and I never lied again. Remember, a liar must be careful destroy the evidence – and needs a good memory.'

14

I first heard this on the evening of the bonbon theft! It did the trick, but I preferred my stories in books.

After we moved to Gipsy Road Dad graduated to restaurant management, with Mum helping him out at weekends. Next door to the Odeon in Bexleyheath Broadway, it was probably more a greasy spoon café than a restaurant, with perhaps one waitress and a cook for Dad to 'manage.' It was reached up a dimly lit, uncarpeted flight of stairs. On Saturdays Mum would put me to bed with the usual warning to be a good girl,
'Uncle John will be there to look after you.'

'Uncle John' was a lodger who slept in the spare bedroom. One Saturday evening I couldn't get to sleep; it was still daylight and there was no sign of Uncle John. I hated being alone in the house, knew about buses and where the café was, so I took the fare money from my moneybox and walked up the road, over the bridge across the railway. I passed a man I thought was Uncle John but he didn't notice me. He'd probably forgotten what I looked like, we didn't meet very often and I think Mum usually left me asleep, knowing John would be back soon. Child care was very ad hoc and a child once put to bed was considered safely out of the way, but this six-year-old was adventurous.

I climbed upstairs on the red trolleybus, which for my short legs was like mountaineering. Why the conductor didn't question a small girl asking for a ticket to the Odeon I have no idea. Perhaps he did. I must have seemed very sure of my destination and he may have waited to see me walk up the stairs to the Café. I was already wondering how much trouble I would be in. They must have been shocked to see me, but surprisingly, instead of a reprimand I was given eggs and bacon and told how clever I was to find my way there, though I must never do anything like that again. I wonder what they said to Uncle John?

The visit to the cinema on my fifth birthday had heralded a lifetime love of film and theatre. It was cemented at the Granada Cinema, Welling which opened to a loud fanfare in February 1938, a few days after my 7th birthday. I went with my friend Audrey Walden to the Saturday morning Children's Club where we cheered on the Lone Ranger and Tonto, Gene Autry and Tarzan or laughed at the Three Stooges, Laurel and Hardy and Will Hay. A year later the Saturday Club was invited to the cinema's first Anniversary party, with a huge birthday cake in the foyer. We were each given a slice of cake and a drink, found our classmates and settled down noisily to the film, talking and giggling more than would ever have been condoned in school. Our applause was long and loud, I'm sure we thought the film stars could hear us. Dad had convinced me there were people in our wireless, but they disappeared before I could ever get round to the back and see them.

After the film there was a drum roll; not real drums, just the sound. A voice boomed from the darkness::
'Quiet now, boys and girls, settle down and wait for Uncle Robbie.'
A loud noise, flashing lights and a huge Wurlitzer organ rose up from under the stage, a smiling man in a white suit turning towards us without taking his hands off the keys. This was Robinson Cleaver, who appeared and disappeared several times a day and whose face beamed down from a poster outside the Granada. He played two songs, we sang 'Happy Birthday, dear Granada' and the organ disappeared under the stage. There was time for another film, then off home. The Granada introduced me to Dorothy Lamour in 'The Road to Morocco,' and I longed to be old enough to wear a sarong and perhaps swing in trees.

February 1938 was significant for an even more exciting event than the opening of the Granada. My cousin Veronica was born at our house a few days before my birthday. Auntie Doll and Uncle Ernie came over with Doreen and Pat, my favourite cousins, but after tea the girls went off somewhere else.
Auntie Doll was very fat, and Mum said
'Be careful not to hit Auntie Doll's tummy, it's sore.'
I had no intention of doing so, but was used to weird instructions.
I wasn't too happy about letting Auntie Doll have my bed, but she was going to get a baby and wanted to be somewhere comfortable when it arrived. Would it come down the chimney? It wasn't Christmas, but no-one had said Santa Claus would be bringing the baby, so that didn't really matter. Next morning a nurse arrived and I had to take Uncle Ernie for a walk. Mum said
'She'll start yelling soon, he's better off out of it.'
We went to Danson Park but Uncle Ernie soon ran out of cigarettes. He was smoking Woodbines non-stop, so we went to buy more, then he wanted to go straight home.
Mum opened the door, all smiles.
'Another girl!'
But he didn't seem very pleased. He said

'She says that's her lot, so I shan't be getting a boy.'
Why were boys always so important?
'We're calling her Veronica so she can be Ron and I'll teach her to kick a ball about.'

I was taken upstairs to see the new baby and wished very hard that I could have a sister. It was useless, I would always be an only child, but there were cousins galore. Doreen, Pat and Veronica were my favourites. They lived in Erith and Auntie Doll had lots of sisters who lived nearby. They, with their children, came in and out of the cousins' house all the time. There was always noise and fun there, not like at home, where I had to be quiet and play by myself. They must have been quite poor, supper was often cornflakes and warm milk in white pudding basins, not quite as nice as the thin sandwiches my mother made, but Auntie Doll allowed us to lick the basins. Uncle Bill, Dad's next brother down after Uncle Ernie, had a boy, Ronald and there was a cousin Harry too, whose Mum was Dad's big sister Ethel. Harry was much older than me and I didn't know him very well. Dad's youngest brother was Jack, but he was still too young to be married.

My eighth birthday party was a disappointment. I was used to never winning the Pass the Parcel, which meant Mum must have cheated, but I naively thought it sheer chance. This year Mum had made cards to stick on our backs, with names to guess, like Mr Thomas our Headmaster, Snow White, Goldilocks, Desperate Dan, Dennis the Menace. Mum saw me peeping at the top card.
'That's cheating. You'll have to stand and watch, we can't have cheats joining in.'

She probably saw it as not showing favouritism but for me it was another example of the unfairness of life. It *was* my birthday and I hadn't really cheated, I'd seen only one name. Adults' arbitrary rules fostered a hidden resentment which permeated much of my childhood.

THE WORLD ERUPTS

An evening in the summer of 1939. I'm with Mum and Dad in a smoky over-crowded classroom, adults and children sitting, standing, wandering around examining coloured pictures, charts headed 'History,' 'Geography,' lists of words in a language I don't know. Although it's years away I know about 'big school' and have imagined classrooms but not as smoky as this and with fewer grownups. We're quieter than usual, not just because we're with parents and on our best behaviour. Something is definitely wrong. Not that anything is different at home, I still get told off most days, Mum and Dad grumble at the News on the wireless and at each other. This evening they've brought me to this school.

'Don't wander around, you'll get lost. Sit quietly and read your book.' From habit, I do, though Mum usually complains that I've always got my head in a book. She calls me precocious, I'm not sure what it means but I do love reading and I'm allowed to get books from the library. I'm not enjoying the one about a girl called Pollyanna. The fascinating things on the walls will have to wait, I can't go and look at them but I can't concentrate on my book. Instead I watch some of the other children pulling weird masks over their heads, their eyes hidden behind goggles like Dad wears on his motorbike, but with snouts, a bit like pigs. Some of the children cry, try to snatch them off; one boy is sick down his blazer but his mother isn't cross. I ask a question, Mum says
'Shush, you'll find out in good time, there's a good girl.'
Here we go again, the reminder that being good is the only thing that matters, when I've often no idea why what I've done is bad. Perhaps that's why I don't like Pollyanna, she's always a smiling goody-goody.

My turn to stand by the table piled with masks. They can't be toys, toys aren't this dull grey, children don't cry when they are given them. I'm not sure I want one.
'Off you go. Now don't make a fuss and show me up.'
Up where? I bite my lip; words again. Will it be like the dentist? Mum said the same thing then and afterwards said I was a good girl, because I didn't cry even though it hurt when the needle went into my gum. When Mum took me back to school so I needn't miss any lessons the class clapped me, so I know for sure that not crying is part of being good. I dawdle as slowly as I dare to the table; the man looks kind.

'Margaret Lorraine Fairman? And you're eight and a half?'
How does he know my whole name? And how old I am? Awed into silence, I nod
'Don't worry, we'll make sure one of these fits you, then you can take it home in a box.'
'Why? It's not my birthday. It isn't a toy is it?'
No. my love, it's a.... '
'It looks a bit like Mickey Mouse.'
'That's right. Stand quite still. Can you take a deep breath for me?'
Holding our breaths is a game I play with Lennie next door; he usually wins but I am getting better. One day I'll beat him. The mask smells horribly of rubber but it's fun looking through the eyepieces. He says
'Let your breath out now dear. Is it comfy, not too tight?'
'No – I mean yes thank you.'
The words sound odd, trapped inside the snout. I nod.
'Now turn your head both ways. There's a clever girl.'
He pulls the mask gently off, snout first and presses a damp cloth into my hand.
'Wipe the inside and keep it in this box I've written your name on. Your mummy will find somewhere to put it safe. Here's a sweetie for being good. Off you go now.' And back I go, the cardboard box with its thick cord slung across my body like a giant purse.
I've managed to be both good *and* clever. Mum and Dad are both smiling; I get a brief cuddle.
'Let's get you home to bed; you can say an extra prayer, that you never need to wear the dreadful thing.'
'What's it for, Mummy?'
'You ask too many questions.'

On the way home Dad buys an Evening News and over his shoulder I read the headlines: *'Immediate Issue of Gas Masks to Children. War imminent. '*
Is that the thing in the box? I'm not sure what 'imminent' means, but will I have to wear it whenever Mum or Gran light the cooker? I haven't before.
The boys at school play at soldiers, shooting with their fingers, falling down and rolling around the playground in pretend wars. Are the grownups going to play soldiers too? My friends and I prefer skipping, hopscotch, turning somersaults on the grass.

On Sunday morning September 3 – I know the date because I look at the calendar in the kitchen every day - I'm standing at the front gate of 116 Gipsy Road with Mum, Dad and Gran, a peculiar wailing sound

all around us. When it began the kettle was on the boil and Mum has made a pot of tea. A man with a light-brown voice said on the wireless a few minutes ago
'This country is at war with Germany.'

The grownups have brought their cups of tea with them. People have stayed home from church to hear Mr Chamberlain, the brown-voiced man, others have gone with frail hopes to pray for peace. Neighbours peer through curtains or like us, stand at front gates, some lugging cardboard boxes containing those funny masks.
One man wears a tin hat; a woman is crying, a noise foreign to this street where people keep to themselves
'Looks quiet enough to me.'
That's Dad. Mum says
'Perhaps they're only practising.'
That's when I put in my bit,
'Are they only practising a war?'
As usual, they laugh at me. Half indulgent, half sarcastic with this slip of a child, blue overall covering pink Sunday dress, matching pink bow in my hair, white ankle socks ('careful not to dirty them'), brown Clarks sandals.
'Our Margaret's always got an answer.'

I've been kept home from Sunday school 'In case.' In case what? What will 'War' mean? Is it the tin Anderson shelter dug into my father's precious lawn, his pride in the storage seats he's built inside, filled with mugs, a teapot, packets of food, a playhouse for me and Lennie? My Uncle Bill is going off to the army. Will my cousin Phil go too, or worse, my Dad? There are two more uncles, Ernie and Jack and my cousin Harry. I hear Mum tell someone both Uncle Charlies are too old and Dad might just get away with it. This is puzzling. Soldiers are brave, aren't they – doesn't Mum want Dad to be brave? We go indoors, the grownups arguing over whether I will be going away. Not into the army, I hope.

Mum says
'Nearly time to go back to school, supposing it opens.'
Mass evacuation of schools had begun in the summer holidays, Mr Chamberlain's statement was not news to those in charge. My class had already left, though Mum didn't tell me. Four or five of us still at home, possibly with anxious parents who wouldn't trust strangers, went to school on the first day of term but were sent home. After that we met for lessons every morning in our house with Miss Kingsley,

our teacher. If the sirens went, which was rarely, we scrambled under the dining table, making it seem like a game. I've no idea if we were learning much but I enjoyed those weeks before Mum told me to choose one doll and two books, as well as my teddy, to take on a train with her to Stamford, where we often spent holidays with my great aunts, Aunt Bess and Aunt Annie. Great Uncle Frank, Aunt Annie's husband lived there too, but his loud, miserable voice scared me and I avoided him whenever I could.

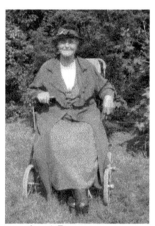

Aunt Bess   *Aunt Annie and Uncle Frank*

Mum said I was going to be a 'private' evacuee in a house near the Great-aunts. A back alley separated the Great-Aunts' house from an identical terrace where I was to stay with Mr and Mrs Rice and Doris, who was fourteen. When Mum took me across to their house Doris held out her hand and took me upstairs to my bedroom. I think it used to be hers. She'd put out a grocer's and a butcher's shop, scale models of Victorian interiors with toy food and a cash register for me to play with. Treasures more wonderful than any toys I'd ever had, except my teddy, who slept on my pillow until I went back to London. I became Doris's slave; fortunately she was very tolerant. Mum and Mrs Rice must both have welcomed this arrangement, Mum because I was going to a family known to her Aunts, guaranteed to be clean; Mrs Rice relieved to have a recommended child. She would have heard tales of bedwetting, nit-prone, foulmouthed 'cockney kids.' Families who took in genuine evacuees, whether privately or 'bulk delivery' Londoners were paid 10 shillings a week (about £75 now.)

I learned to live with hissing gas lamps with thin white covers over the flames, called mantles, which crumbled and broke easily once they burned out. They were a bit like spiders' webs and had to be lit with a match. Mrs Rice called her kitchen the 'scullery.' The shallow yellow sink and stone floor, the weird stone contraption, called a copper, jutting out from one corner were like nothing I'd ever seen. Mrs Rice lit a fire underneath the copper on Mondays, heating water to do the laundry. On Fridays there was more hot water, scooped out into a tin bath for first Doris, then me to have our weekly scrub beside the black-leaded range in the living room. Mr Rice would go out for a beer with the lads on Friday evenings, perhaps to spare blushes all round. I don't know when the adults bathed, unless on Fridays after we were safely in bed. The toilet was outside in the yard, dark and unlit, with a wooden bench seat.

The day I arrived the table was piled with 'High tea,' regular Saturday fare in the Rice household. Pork pie, (Stamford is still famous for its pork butchers), salad, sandwiches, home-made cakes and scones. Mum seldom found time to bake cakes. Nothing was rationed yet, but I'd heard Mum say that shelves in the shops near us in London were almost empty.

The Rice family continued my film education. Every Saturday night they took Doris to the cinema and I suppose they took me along with them so she didn't have to forgo the outing and look after me (babysitting was not in any dictionary in 1939). I was bewitched by the first film I saw, 'In Old Chicago,' falling hopelessly in love with the brooding and handsome Tyrone Power. At home I'd been taken to see Shirley Temple at our local cinema in Bexleyheath. I was glad I didn't have such tight curls as hers, but I loved singing 'The Good Ship Lollipop.' I'd seen 'Snow White' too, as well as going regularly to the Saturday morning club at the Granada, but these were children's films. In Stamford I saw Judy Garland and Mickey Rooney in Andy Hardy films and the luscious Deanna Durbin and many handsome male film stars.

Any tendency towards homesickness vanished with these delights. First, high tea, always pork pie and salad, cakes and possibly jelly, then a walk down Cheyne Lane, a very narrow lane, almost a passage with shops on one side, to a sweetshop. We would choose our favourites, mine were aniseed balls and pear drops, and suck our way through two films and British Movietone News. I became an avid reader of Picture Show and Film Pictorial, two magazines Doris collected and a fan of Beano and Film Fun, far more interesting than Enid Blyton's Sunny Stories, which I read every week at home.

On that first weekend Mum stayed with her aunts but she came for Saturday tea with the Rice family and left me there to unpack. On Sunday she knocked at the Rice back door and collected me for church. In the middle of a hymn she grabbed my hand so hard it hurt. I peeped at her and she was crying, which was worrying. As we walked back to my new home Mum talked non-stop
'You can go in and see Aunt Bess whenever you want, but ask Mrs Rice first and be a good girl and don't forget to say your prayers and clean your teeth and say please and thank you.'

Not Aunt Annie or Uncle Frank, Aunt Bess was the one who mattered to Mum. When she was my age Mum and Uncle Charles would spend summer holidays with Aunt Bess and her husband Uncle Robby, who died before I was born. Aunt Bess had a terrible accident when I was a few weeks old, when she fell under a horse-drawn brewers' dray. One leg had to be amputated and the other was badly injured, so she spent the rest of her life in a wheelchair or walking round the house with two sticks. Perhaps it hurt and that was what made her so bad-tempered most of the time.

I was not particularly sad about Mum going. I was used being looked after by Gran while Mum was at work and Aunt Bess was Gran's sister, so I swiftly transferred to her the half-affection, half-fear my Gran inspired. I was happy with the Rice family and felt no need to seek the refuge I suspect Mum was hinting at.

On Monday Mrs Rice took me to my new school, All Saints. The building was nothing like Brampton Road, but a Victorian Church school with classrooms divided by folding partitions and a huge stove in the middle which warmed both us and our mid-morning milk. The lavatories were in the playground. I would wait until it was almost too late, to avoid the cold and the smells. So in Stamford it was not just houses which had outside toilets. I thought only London houses had bathrooms.

I spent only a few weeks at All Saints before Mum decided I was going home for Christmas. She wrote every week, her copperplate handwriting offering cheerful news of Gran and Dad and saying she missed me. I never heard from Dad, he never wrote letters to anyone. Going home was a further great adventure, travelling alone on a coach to Victoria Coach Station, where Mum would meet me. Mr and Mrs Rice took me to the coach stop, where I was most disappointed. Trains had coaches, so why wasn't this one as long as a train?

Mr Rice asked the driver to look after me. Why? It was only a sort of single-decker bus, there was no corridor to walk along and the door would be closed. I was unlikely to leap from the window or hide in the luggage rack, all I had to do was sit still with my teddy and read my book. Trains had 'Ladies Only' carriages, Gran usually sat in one. She said it was safer. So was being on a coach or a train with men not safe? I'd never seen a 'Men only' carriage.

Someone spoke to Mr Rice.

'I'll look after her and I'll make sure she gets delivered to her Mum.' She was beautiful, like a doll, with a head of glorious yellow bubble curls, a fur coat and, most exciting of all, red shoes. Mrs Rice looked a little worried; was it the red shoes? The driver winked.

'We'll get the little lass there in one piece, between us.'

'There's room next to me; sit by the window. What's your name, me duck?'

I've never forgotten those curls.

The December light was fading and I wondered how long the journey would be. The signs saying how far to London were painted over. We went past Burghley House, the Bottle Lodges we'd often passed on Sunday walks after church definitely bottle-shaped. Mrs Rice allowed no toys or sewing on Sundays, only church and walks, though I was allowed a book for an hour at bedtime. And now I was going home.

The driver called

'Attention, please. Pull all the blackout blinds down so I can switch the lights on.'

Then I heard a whispered

'Wake up, kiddo, it's teatime.'

Tea time? I'd not long had my dinner. Had I really slept? The coach had stopped outside a dark building. Nothing strange there, all buildings were blacked out after dark.

'Where are we?'

Kidnap, bandits, German spies. Books were all very well, but they gave me ideas.

'It's called Biggleswade, the coach stops here for a break. Hold my hand so you don't trip.'

First stop inside the restaurant was the Ladies, which I certainly needed. For what seemed hours I watched fascinated as this vision applied scarlet lipstick and teased out every bubbly curl with a tail-comb, an implement I'd never seen before. I felt the first cravings for the wonders of growing up, choosing my own hairstyle and clothes. Eventually she was satisfied and we found a table.

'My treat' she said 'What would you like, me duck?'
The familiar Lincolnshire endearment. Brought up not to be greedy, I asked for a cake and lemonade.
'Are you sure?'
When her plate of scrambled eggs arrived I regretted my frugal choice. I loved scrambled eggs and we didn't often have them. They were a bit scarce in the shops and Mrs Rice used her eggs for cakes. Perhaps there were hens in the garden of this Biggleswade café. I crumbled my slice of cake, imagining the taste of those golden yolks.

It was dark when we reached Victoria and I wondered how Mum would find me in the blackout. A woman wearing a dark coat and a wide-brimmed green hat was standing near the coach stop. It was Mum; she held me very tight and smiled and smiled, not forgetting to remind me to thank my friend and to hope I had been good.
'Very good,'
Bubble curls said. I'd forgotten how important being good was for Mum, it hadn't been quite such a burden while I was with the Rice family. But for today I'd managed it.
Dad was waiting at home; he gave me a quick hug, ruffled my hair and said
'Time for bed, littl'un'. You can have a biscuit with cocoa tonight for a treat. '
I was definitely back home.

SO THIS IS PROPER WAR

There was very little enemy action. Brampton Road School was still open and I joined the many 'private' evacuees like me who were returning. Lenny still lived next door and as they didn't have an Anderson shelter we played at air raids in ours, spending most Saturdays in my back garden. I was glad to see all my cousins again and soon forgot Stamford, though at Christmas I'd been cruelly disappointed. I'd asked for a model shop like those Doris had. Santa brought a tiny cardboard shop-front filled with disproportionately large bottles of highly perfumed sweets. Doris's shops were scale models of Victorian interiors. Wartime austerity may have explained the discrepancy, but it was the first of many presents which were never quite what I'd asked for.

Most weekends we saw aunts and uncles. One Saturday Uncle Bill came to tea on his own in his soldier's uniform.

'Muriel's sick, she's expecting,' he said.

If I was expecting something, like a birthday, I'd often get so excited I felt sick, but I didn't know grownups were the same. Uncle Bill gave me a shilling when he went but Dad made me hand it back.

'It's nearly a day's pay' he told his brother, 'You can't spare that.'

He told me to give my uncle a very big kiss as he was going off to fight. The 'fight' was Dunkirk, where Uncle Bill was taken prisoner, though my parents' friend Wally was rescued. There was a party when Uncle Wally came home and I was allowed to stay up, but it was only grownups with drinks getting very noisy. We were staying at Uncle Wally and Aunty Kay's house and I asked to go to bed. They forgot to put the light out, so I read for hours. Biggles was my favourite, or the Just William books; there were no Worrals of the WAAF books for another year.

Soon the Blitz and the Battle of Britain began and every night we took sandwiches and flasks of tea down to the Anderson shelter, where we would stay even though there were sometimes no air raids. It was difficult to sleep, the bench seats were narrow and hard, but being hit by a bomb would have been far worse. Gran was now living with us but refused to come into the shelter with us.

'If I'm going to be killed it will be in my own bed. Or my armchair. Not down a hole.'

Lenny and I often played in the garden during daytime air raids, counting planes as they fell, sorting out Heinkels from Messerschmitts and sadly the occasional Spitfire or Hurricane. One day the man on the wireless announced that nearly 200 German planes had been shot down. On Saturday the glow of fires from the sugar refineries across the Thames at Silvertown and from Woolwich Arsenal was like the best sunset ever.

People began to be really worried. Dad had bad legs and was medically unfit to be called up, so he drove lorries loaded with ammunition to Army posts in the north. He was usually away for half the week but came home for the weekends. In November, a few weeks after the Woolwich raid, Dad was in Coventry the morning after it was bombed. When he came home I saw him cry for the first time ever. He held me on his knee, cuddling me so tight it hurt and said things like

'Kids looking for their Mums, people queuing at pumps, filthy, covered in soot, digging in piles of bricks. Firemen crying over those pitiful little bodies.'

That night he decided the family had to leave London.

'Running away then?'

Mrs Allen, Len's mummy, wasn't being very nice, but Lennie was crying and I think she was cross because I was going away again and he was upset.

Dad risked taking us as passengers on his next journey, which was to Scotland. The lorry had a thick steel panel between the driving part and the back where the ammunition was stored. Mum perched in front between Dad and his 'convoy,' the extra driver. Dad concealed Gran and me in the back of the lorry, warning us, me in particular

'This is dangerous. If you move you'll blow us all to smithereens, so you mustn't make a sound. Don't fidget, sit still, both of you. And be good, littl'un.'

The doors were fastened with a loud bang which made me jump and Gran and I were left in pitch dark.

I'd seen explosions on the newsreels and was terrified by the idea of becoming smithereens. I can still feel the cold, hard edges of the metal boxes pressing into my thighs, my poor teddy squashed in my arms. I panicked if Gran coughed or even whispered to me. The journey to Stamford seemed to last forever, there was no stopover for tea at Biggleswade like we'd had on the coach journey last Christmas. Dad must have been scared too, mainly of being caught. The inch thick steel 'safety' shield would be pretty useless if the load did blow up, yet he'd left me sitting directly on top of the ammunition. As he rarely acknowledged Gran's existence, her safety didn't count.

It was dark when we finally arrived and the Great Aunts had no idea we were coming, so no beds or food were prepared. I was apparently so rigid with cold and tension that I had to be carried into the house and was unable to empty my bladder for two days. I doubt if I saw a doctor, it would have cost money and how would anyone dare to explain why I'd got into such a state?

I was fortunately young enough not to understand the major horrors of war. Documentaries say how scared children were, but the film-makers can't have spoken to anyone I knew. Apart from the lorry incident, which for me was less about war than the fear of massacring my family, it was almost a game, the guns and searchlights on Shooters Hill as exciting to watch as fireworks nights. Perhaps we were displacing our fears. It took the Korean War in 1950, when many of the boys we'd known at school might have to spend their National Service genuinely fighting and perhaps being killed, to give me some understanding of how parents must have hidden their fears from their children whenever possible.

A year or so later I saw Dad cry for a second time. His youngest brother Jack, who was his extra driver that week on the ammunition lorry, was late for work so they missed the opportunity for Saturday overtime. Dad was furious with him, I heard them shouting. The lorry was blown to pieces near Kings Cross and no trace of their mates' bodies was found. Feelings, especially men's feelings, were disguised as jokes

'If your name's not on it, you're OK.'

But it was no longer a joke when your name, not your friends' should have been written on the bombs.

After a few days at the Aunts' house Mum, Gran and I went to stay in a cramped terraced house with quite an old lady called Mrs Lank. I expect having three extra people, including a child, was too much for her and we soon moved to the Stag and Pheasant, a noisy and possibly disreputable pub in Broad Street. Mrs Jeffcoate, the landlady, was a widow. We 'lived in' as family, with Mum and me in a room where we shared a double bed and another room for Gran. Dad usually stayed overnight on his way to or from delivering ammunition and then I had to share Gran's bed, which I hated. She smelt stale and woke me when she kept getting up to use the chamber pot which was kept under the bed. Dad had brought some of my toys up, so as well as my teddy I now had my two dolls, a large white one which wore real baby's clothes and a black one, Sammy. Most of my friends had black dolls. We were not bothered that they resembled no-one we had seen outside picture books.

The Stag and Pheasant Stamford

A former coaching inn dating back to1663, now a listed building, the Stag & Pheasant had a large yard and outbuildings, formerly stables, which had been rebuilt as toilets with proper china lavatories and washbasins. They were filthy at weekends, with vomit which often spilled outside. I would have to tread carefully and not play ball there until the pot-man had swilled down the yard.

The pub was next door to the Catholic Church and on Sunday mornings there would be a queue waiting for opening time. Good Irish Catholics working at the many aerodromes surrounding Stamford, they would attend Mass a few hours after depositing much of their beer in the pub yard before staggering back to the 'digs' they called home to sleep, then back to the pub, eager to fill up again and possibly leave even more behind. Such scenes may have been a factor in my as yet barely conscious mistrust both of alcohol and of religious hypocrisy.

STAMFORD SECOND TIME AROUND

Back to All Saints School. I'd forgotten how different it was from Brampton Road, I'd spent only a few weeks there during my first stay in Stamford. This time eight of us, all 'private' evacuees, were herded into a group in the playground, while the other children lined up and stared at us. It was taken for granted that we eight would be friends, though all we had in common was our evacuee status. I think it must have been a girls' only school as I don't remember any boys. First we were given tests, which I discovered were to allocate our seats. Every Friday the whole school was tested and some children moved up or down. The front right-hand double desk was for the two top girls and the back left-hand one for the 'stupid.' The top seats always belonged to Jocelyn Harris and Anne Hartley but fortunately, knowing Mum's sharp tongue and her expectations I spent most of my time in fourth or fifth place.

Partitions dividing the classrooms were pulled open daily to form a hall for Assembly. My main memories of All Saints are of bottles of milk warming and often turning sour on the stove which heated the whole school and comforted frozen hands (though not stomachs) on cold mornings; the cold and often smelly toilets and the weekly visit from the white-robed Vicar, with his injunctions to be good (nothing new there, then) his oily voice reading endless Bible stories as he walked round the room, patting us on the shoulder. I hated him.

Life in the pub was not without its tensions. Mrs Jeffcoate would quarrel regularly with Julie, her daughter. At least, I thought she was her daughter, until I heard Mrs J. shout
'You're no daughter of mine.'
But she was, wasn't she? Julie was also
'No better than she should be.'
I thought this was high praise, surely you had only to be good, no need to be better than that, but it didn't sound like it when Mrs J shouted at Julie. Her crime? She'd produced a baby, also named Julie, the father unknown but likely to be an American G.I. Julie's current boyfriend Jim, a gentle and sober Irish air gunner who sang to both baby Julie and her mum, was told by Mrs J.
'You're a fool if you marry a slut like my daughter.'
Marry her he did, only to be killed in action three months later. I was too young to appreciate that Julie's baby could now be called legitimate; not officially adopted but with a real 'Daddy,' even if he

was a dead one. There was no longer any need for Mrs J. to hang her head in shame.

There were some unpleasant times for me. Children were allowed in the Bar only if they were related to employees. As Mum served behind the Saloon Bar I often wandered around, unnoticed by her as I was grabbed for an uncomfortable cuddle by some of the customers. I had my bottom pinched, my cheeks and often lips dampened with beery kisses. Mum didn't seem to see, but child molestation was rarely acknowledged, or often dismissed as harmless fun.

The attic in the roof space was a treasure house, its window covered with thick blackout blinds. One bare bulb created mysterious shadows behind boxes, jars, bottles, discarded junk, old clothes and bits of broken furniture. Our suitcases were up there too, with precious things like Mum's wedding veil and orange blossom headdress which Dad had brought to Stamford for safe keeping. I would dress up in it, fill jars with water, cook imaginary meals for imaginary friends. I heard Mum tell Mrs J.
'Don't know why she spends so much time up there, it's such a mess. Still, it keeps her quiet.'

I joined the Brownies and later the Guides. On my way home from Guides it was my job to buy fish and chips for supper. The blackout meant shop doors had to be kept closed, opening only to disgorge one customer and let in the next, releasing warm smells that made me hungry. One evening an airman in front of me turned round and smiled. I smiled back, Mum had taught me to be polite. She'd also told me never on any account to talk to strangers, but I wasn't exactly talking to him, and if he was a stranger why would he smile? He must be someone who came into the pub.

The queue was moving slowly. Lots of food was rationed now, but not fish or potatoes. Mr and Mrs Hardy, who owned the shop, were 'making a packet out of the war.'
A packet of what? No-one ever explained. The airman left.
My turn.
'Fish and chips three times, please.'
Someone pushed me; not quite pushing but stroking my bottom. How rude. Someone from Guides? Turning, I bumped my nose on the brass button of an RAF greatcoat.
'Hello dear,' he murmured.
I nearly dropped the money as I went to pay. Mrs Hardy frowned.
'You all right, love? You look a bit pale. Mind you go straight home.'

I wasn't all right, not at all, but I didn't say anything. I knew something was wrong. This must be what Mum's warnings were about, the man was a stranger, not the kind of person to smile at. I ran up Broad Street but got out of breath and had to slow down. I could hear boots clumping behind me. What had Mum said?

'If you are ever worried about the dark, ask a grownup if you can walk with them.'

But if I wasn't allowed to speak to strangers how could I decide which grownups were helpful or which ones might be frightening, like the airman? Four people were walking up Broad Street and I walked beside them, not too near but close enough to stop the man making a sudden grab.

Crying now, I reached The Stag at last. When Mum saw me she put her hands on my shoulders.

'Stop crying and tell me what's the matter.'

'Th-th-there was a man, he touched.....'

Mum vanished, but soon burst back into the room.

'He must have turned back when you came in here. What did he ... What did you...?'

Then, words I so rarely heard

'You were a good girl. Come on, let's go and wash your face. You can have extra chips, then I'll tuck you up in bed and read to you.'

In February 1941 we 'sat the Scholarship.' Another mystery. We sat every school day at uncomfortable twin desks where our knees were squashed. On this special occasion the only difference was that we had a whole desk to ourselves. We'd been practising for ages with tests. Mum nagged me not to let my pen drip ink all over the page. A scholarship would get me to a better senior school. I passed.
I don't think I would have dared to fail, but going to the High School did not automatically follow. Apparently my local authority was still Kent. There were letters from Maidstone about fees, muttered arguments when Dad came to visit on his way to and from Yorkshire. Mum told me that being an evacuee meant the scholarship didn't work in Stamford and Dad wasn't going to pay fees, even if he could have afforded it. I had no idea what that meant, but was disappointed that I wouldn't after all be going to the grey stone building halfway up St Martins. Instead I went to the Fane, the local elementary school where I met Josie Sibson, who became a lifelong friend.

My mother went to see the Headmistress of the Fane, I'm not sure at whose instigation or what was said, but after a month I moved to the High School. Twenty years later, helping Mum clear papers when she sold her house I found a letter from that Headmistress, urging her to 'Allow Margaret to take up the scholarship. It might lead to a very secure position in the Civil Service.'

And so it did. My future decided for me when I was ten.

Mum spent a frantic Saturday buying me the most frugal possible uniform. Clothes rationing had begun in June and she'd stocked up in the spring with knickers, fortunately navy blue though being pocket-less they were not exactly what Stamford High School demanded. I had liberty bodices too (don't ask, they were ugly garments with buttons which held suspenders to keep stockings up); stockings, not quite the correct colour and thickness for SHS and a coat, fortunately navy blue. My outdoor shoes had to pinch my toes for another term, but there were compulsory new plimsolls and house shoes (we had to change our shoes when we took off our coats) which I had to have, but in a size too large. Almost half my annual clothing coupons went on equipping me for my new life, but I didn't care that there would be no new Christmas dress. War meant there wouldn't be much of a Christmas anyway. The shop had run out of ties, so I was not only a late arrival but incompletely dressed.

Starting yet another school was confusing. All the other new girls had learned where classrooms were, that the clanging bell signalled the end of each lesson, that we changed classrooms for different subjects. Then there was homework, which was called Prep; belonging to a House – mine was St Patrick's; learning to play hockey; remembering the teachers' names. The only familiar point was playtime, though I now had to call it 'Break,' where we had the usual milk, colder and fresher than at All Saints and with wonderful sticky buns. What might have been a miserable time was avoided, as Jo Sibson joined me. She'd failed the scholarship but her parents decided at the last minute to pay for her and she was put in my form, Upper III Parallel, mainly for scholarship girls. Upper III was for paying pupils and boarders with posh voices and often sneers at the scholarship girls. I managed to keep up and get good marks for most subjects and discovered that I enjoyed French.

The following year the forms were merged. The more academic among us would be learning Latin and went into Lower 1V Parallel. Our accents had been improved by compulsory Voice Production lessons from Miss Teat. Optional elocution lessons were for private pupils. As a Londoner I had fewer vowels to modify and won a Gold star when telling the story of finding a pigeon with a broken wing and nursing it in a shoebox. The implicit snobbery of these lessons was lost on me at the time, but it was a positive attempt by the school to help us to fit in with the 'posh' girls who joined us in Lower IV Parallel. Clever girls were not expected to cook and only Lower IV had domestic science lessons. Our year of 'Domski' had to wait until Lower V. I still have my book of notes on nutrition and wartime recipes and used to threaten to make the Christmas cake, complete with prunes and carrots, if only I could bear to use dried eggs. We did needlework in that year too, my reports often stating how grubby my work was. No-one seemed to notice that as I was left-handed the overall I was making was upside down and I was working backwards, constantly pulling out stitches.

My Form Mistress, Miss Batty, taught my favourite subject, English. Very sadly she died of cancer at the end of that year and it seemed as if the whole school, though possibly only those she taught, went to her funeral in a packed church. She'd been an inspirational teacher with a permanent influence on me and, I suspect, many others.

Despite clothes rationing we were expected to have a different uniform for the summer term, floral dresses and hideous and ill-fitting panama hats. This must have been doubly difficult for Mum, not only financially but for some reason we were moving back to London, so the whole outfit would be unnecessary once term ended.

The High School, Stamford

BACK TO LONDON AGAIN

The Gipsy Road house had been requisitioned for the duration of the war, so we returned to a rented Victorian house in Watling Street, Bexleyheath, very near Aunt Rose and Uncle Charlie's house on Pinnacle Hill, though my lovely Uncle Charlie had died while we were away. Aunt Rose used to visit nearly every evening, often very upset, crying over tales of flooding and running out of cloths. I was quite surprised that houses on a hill could flood, but with hindsight and more knowledgeable school friends I learned she was probably menopausal, an addition to my vocabulary, though I wasn't supposed to say it aloud. Sanitary wear in wartime was primitive; we used old hand towels or pieces of sheets sewn into squares, folded into triangles with loops then attached to a belt round our waists! They were bulky and uncomfortable and had to be washed and worn again until they were threadbare. We were excused PE on those 'difficult' days. A girl in my form who hated PE was challenged by Miss McBean, the gym mistress
'Your monthlies seem to have lasted for six weeks. Better get someone to take you to the doctor tomorrow. Now - tunic off and get moving.'

I was getting used to living in other people's houses and at least this one had plenty of room. Mum, Gran and I each had a bedroom, Dad of course slept with Mum when he was between journeys. Downstairs there were window shutters, no need for blackout curtains. Making sure the shutters were closed every night was my job, which I took very seriously. We had a garden, a long strip of earth with no flowers and little space to Dig for Victory, but we kept rabbits and chicks. Few of the latter survived to lay eggs. Dad would buy them by the dozen and bring them home in a cardboard box, warming them by the kitchen stove. I hated watching as they staggered and fell, to be scooped up and deposited in the dustbin. Coal was in short supply and the oven provided our only heat, except at weekends when the sitting room fire was lit. That winter I did my homework swaddled in scarves and fingerless gloves, unless I could persuade Mum to let me sit at the kitchen table.
'Don't get your books dirty.'

I found a friend in Mr Boswell, our landlord who lived a few houses along and came to collect the rent every Friday. An old man, with hair Gran called 'salt and pepper' and glasses that looked as if they would fall off his nose at any minute, he'd lost a grandchild in an air raid and Mum said being with me helped him. I liked going to his house, he was kind and gave me two Victorian treasures, one a game of Solitaire in a round wooden tray with holes for the green clay balls, the other a Book of

Games and Pastimes with old-fashioned drawings. I think Mum felt sorry for Mr Boswell and she let me keep them.

Before I started yet another new school Mum promised me a week visiting museums and other famous places in London, her reason
'You seem to be history mad and it'll get that head of yours out of a book for a few hours,'
How else did she think I knew about these places I longed to see? I remember only one day, which may have been the only day we managed, when we met my cousin Philip at Hampton Court. I have no idea how many Museums managed to stay open, but have never forgotten the Maze, Henry VIII's huge chairs and the sandbags round the walls of the Palace. The three of us lunched at the smart hotel opposite – still open, but beyond my price range today. Restaurants were limited to a maximum charge of 5 shillings (25p today), which gave two courses, with bread and coffee as non-optional extras. I expect I chose fish and chips, a perennial favourite, supposing they were available, but it was more likely to have been a version of spam or meat substitute. Whatever the food, I still remember that day.

Mum and Auntie Kay took me to the theatre too. I'd been to the Woolwich Theatre with my parents before the war, to see people like Max Miller who told jokes I think were a bit rude. This time we were to see a musical 'The Maid of The Mountains' at the London Coliseum, with Sonny Hale. He was coincidentally Jessie Matthews' husband, providing a link to my very first film. The plot was irrelevant but the music, the colours, Auntie Kay's generosity in squandering her whole monthly 12 ounce sweet ration which the three of us chewed non-stop stuck in my memory. I am word perfect with 'A bachelor gay am I.'

Time to begin the new term at Dartford County School for Girls. An outsider again, but at least attending on the first day and with the correct uniform, as I'd outgrown my navy blue Stamford tunic and Mum could justify buying a new green one. My blouses were cream rather than white, but they would fit for another year or so. This was more about clothing coupons than meanness or poverty on my mother's part. Barbar Seaton, a friend from Stamford who had come home to Bexleyheath a term earlier, called for me on the first day. She left her bike at my house and we caught a trolley bus, so there was no need for Mum to take me.

Forms at Dartford were numbered by year, so I was now a Third Year rather than Upper IV and pupils were streamed. 3L (Latin), for the academics; next was 3G (German); then 3A, the possible improvers and finally 3B, not-sure-how-this-lot-made-it-to-grammar-school-riff-raff. Barbara and I took it for granted we'd be together in 3L but for some reason, possibly the school was overwhelmed by the numbers of returning evacuees it was obliged to take, I was put in 3B. I was soon bored and became disruptive, sitting at the back of the class, amusing my allies with my great wit. Teachers were less impressed. I had as yet learned neither diplomacy nor to recognise irony and when a maths teacher asked icily

'Is this work too easy for you, Margaret?'

I responded with naive honesty

'Yes miss,'

failing to explain that I'd covered the topic the previous year. A detention for impertinence followed.

National Curricula were non-existent. I have never studied Asia in geography but a double dose of America and Australasia has meant I can still recite details of sheep farming on the Murray Darling Plains in Australia, 'Marketing maize on the hoof' (corned beef) in Mid-western USA and recite South American capital cities. I cannot visualise Japan apart from photos of Hiroshima, or Indian exports and need an atlas to locate Afghanistan or China.

At half-term the Headmistress, Miss Fryer, strode into the classroom and announced I was to move to 3G. She may as well as have said

'Margaret is too clever to be with you lot,'

as unpopularity in both Forms was guaranteed. It was unfair; Barbara was in 3L and she hated Latin.

I was right, no-one wanted to know this upstart who'd been promoted and I was miserable. Together with Brenda Whitmore, another returning evacuee, I had extra German lessons in the lunch hour, but no Latin. 3L was presumably full to overflowing and many progress reports were lost in wartime postal mayhem. My parents did not believe in interfering, teachers knew best.

There were some compensations, I found German easy and enjoyed it; there was yet another brilliant English teacher so it remained my favourite subject. The girl who played the lead in the annual drama production of St Joan intended to become an actress. Her name was Sheila Hancock but she was too senior to acknowledge Third Years.

Unlike Stamford, where we'd had a long and tiring walk to the Burghley Park hockey pitches, Dartford had on-site netball courts and playing fields although, apart from one pitch, the fields had been turned over to Dig for

Victory allotments. We kept rabbits, too, useful for sex and gynaecology lessons, plus many tears when the pets vanished. I swear they returned as school dinners poorly disguised in shepherd's pie, made worse by the addition of parsnips. At least the vegetables were home-grown.

Hormones were stirring, there were 'crushes' at school. I became obsessed with a prefect, Yvonne Salisbury and devastated when she chose to spend an evening with her friend Audrey rather than come to tea at my house. When after Christmas Barbara and I joined the Girl Guides at the local Methodist Church I became equally obsessed with Alan, a buck-toothed Boy Scout of sixteen, who was either very shy or, more probably, embarrassed by this twelve-year-old hanger-on. Confused sexuality or a natural Freudian stage?

Gran was becoming a problem. She had diabetes and Mum had to give her daily injections, which both hated. There were regular arguments and accusations of cruelty which often left Mum in tears. Gran would yell, insisting though this had been Mum's job for years, that she was being poisoned. There was incontinence to deal with too, not just at night, which meant constant scrubbing of floors. She refused to stick to her diet, though at least doughnuts were in short supply in the war. Finally she went into hospital. Mum took me to visit her but children under fourteen were not allowed on the wards. The ward Sister was adamant so I was hastily removed and never saw Gran again. I stayed home during evening visiting hours. Dad was mostly away so I would be alone during air raids and very scared. I heard voices in the house, imagining invading Germans with machine guns, only to discover when I tiptoed out to the bathroom that it was the radio in the next room. I never told Mum, there was no point in inviting the usual injunction not to be silly.

I didn't go to the funeral either. Gran had few friends and her sisters in Stamford would have found the journey too difficult in wartime, so only Uncle Charles and his family came. She couldn't be buried near my Grandpa, suicides were put in unmarked graves kept apart from the main cemetery. So many people were dying, soldiers in battles, civilians, many of them children from bombs, that death and funerals were almost everyday occurrences. I imagine no-one thought to include me in this one. Gran stayed a kind of ghost we rarely mentioned after she died. Everything she owned was in her cramped bedroom; I suppose it now belonged to Mum and Uncle Charles. Mum gave me two lurid religious tales Gran often asked me to read to her, 'A Peep Behind the Scenes' and 'Christie's Old Organ.' I asked if I could have a small turquoise glass cradle I'd always loved; I knew I would keep it forever.

Newspapers and the radio were reporting that the war tide was turning, but as a burgeoning adolescent my interests were more self-centred. Apart from homework and Guides I went as often as possible to the cinema. There were fewer air raids and I was definitely too young for dance halls. I was, however, preparing myself. Victor Sylvester would give dancing lessons on the wireless and I would step round the dining room chanting 'Slow, slow, quick, quick, slow,' imagining I now knew how to dance a quickstep.

'Gone With the Wind' was the film of the season, but it was a category 'A' (children under 16 to be accompanied by an adult) so I had to ask someone to take me in with them. People were used to this, we'd been warned never to ask a man who was on his own and we always showed the ticket money clutched in our hands. It was how I'd seen 'Snow White.' Attendants turned a blind eye and once we were inside we sat where we liked. We seemed to be in no danger of abduction or worse and parents were glad to be rid of us for a few hours. I'd made a few friends and at weekends we would cycle to Woolwich Ferry and cross the Thames to ride past the bomb damage in East Ham on the north bank, the boat ride making it far more interesting than our local devastation.

There were no domestic science lessons at Dartford, partly because of rationing, but I was learning to cook at home. One evening I made a surprise supper. Dad was back for a few days and took Mum out for a drink and I used a whole week's cheese ration to make Welsh rarebit. Fortunately it tasted good and Mum could find nothing to complain about, though she couldn't resist
'You should have asked before you used all the cheese.'
For once Dad defended me
'Leave the kid alone, she wanted to surprise us. Good on you, girl.'
Praise so rare I never forgot it.

Rumours were circulating that invasion, this time from our side of the Channel, was imminent. On the morning of June 6 1944 I was getting ready for school, trying to wash in a small bowl of warm water. Every surface was covered with kettles, jugs, saucepans, pudding basins, anything that would hold water as the water mains had been bombed the previous night. I'd heard a car go by as I was falling asleep, broadcasting a warning to collect as much water as possible. Dad was away and Mum had filled everything she could before the pipes ran dry. It had to be used sparingly, which meant a 'lick and a promise' in Mum's leftover soapsuds.

'Mum, can I …?'

'Sh! Listen to this.'

The News on the Home Service told us British troops had landed in Normandy.

'Won't be long now,' Mum said, 'War's almost over. No more air raids.'

How wrong she was.

Later that summer a new and terrifying campaign began – V1s and V2s, known as 'doodlebugs' or 'buzz bombs.' V stood for *vergeltung*, meaning retribution or 'getting our own back.' They were pilotless planes launched on the French coast and landing, when their engines cut out, to explode wherever they fell. If they stopped overhead you were safe, as they travelled another three miles or so before they landed, but there were no other warnings – air raid sirens became useless.

Dad built a Morrison shelter, (named after the Home Secretary, Herbert Morrison) in the kitchen. Constructed in very heavy green steel, it took up most of the space. We were meant to sleep in it but as it was cramped and uncomfortable, like most people we stayed in our beds and used the shelter as a table.

At school we spent most of the day in deep trenches with wooden planks placed on top of banks of earth for seating. I remember 5th Years taking School Certificate exams with papers balanced on their laps and one teacher, Miss Carter, down on her knees praying as we heard loud explosions overhead. We were anxious as we caught our buses home. The more dramatic among us wondered if we might be blown to pieces before we arrived at our destinations.

One morning I had a dentist's appointment. As the dentist went to jab the injection into my gum a plane stopped overhead. Startled, he jumped and jabbed the needle very deep into a nerve. I jumped too, but from pain and panic. The next day my gum became inflamed and I completely went to pieces, refusing to go to school, begging to stay in the Morrison shelter. I rarely came out at all, waiting until the very last minute if I needed the bathroom. My parents were going to Stamford for a holiday to see my Great Aunts and I was meant to stay with my friend Marjorie for a week as term hadn't ended. I was so distressed that they took me with them and so began yet another stay in Stamford. This time we travelled legally and I stayed until well after the war when I left school.

A BRIGHTENING HORIZON?

Returning to Stamford High might have left me feeling self-conscious in my green Dartford uniform, had it not been for a similarly green-uniformed but far more glamorous creature in the year below, her long rope-coloured hair tied back more loosely than school rules allowed. This was Elspeth Ross, who had recently returned from evacuation to Canada. There were no spare clothing coupons for new tunics, so we were forced to stay in our green ones until they could be dyed navy blue, which meant waiting until half-term. Ours were also quite the wrong shape, but Elspeth taught me not to care. The youngest member of a prosperous Stamford family and a budding actor and singer Elspeth, who preferred being called Beth, charmed me and we became 'best buddies' I may have been in the year above but she was only three months younger.

Beth's home, Rock Lodge was my dream house and it was here I knew I wanted one day to live in a similar large, stylish house. It had central heating, six bedrooms, a dining room with an oak dining table large enough for us to play table-tennis, a sitting-room filled with antique furniture, plus a basement kitchen with an Aga and huge refrigerator. Then there was the vast garden. Mr Ross was a Wing Commander and after the war ended, when he was demobilised and came home, Beth and I became his junior staff, expected to spend a half hour on summer evenings dead-heading petunias in one of the flowerbeds. They had a part-time gardener and a live-in housekeeper, a Jewish refugee violinist. Mrs Ross, Beth's mother, welcomed the opportunity very gently to civilise her daughter's new friend. She read poetry to us, to Beth's disgust at her intrusion and my awe that a mother was interested in spending time with her children's friends.

After a year away from SHS I had much catching up to do. The School Certificate syllabus was very different from that in Dartford but I could at least keep most of the subjects, though I had to drop German. Instead I was back to Latin and had extra lessons. I felt that I'd come home. I wasn't a new girl, simply a returner, which happened all the time in the war. The year at Dartford had been difficult, I'd been in two different forms in neither of which I felt comfortable. I became tense and anxious there, possibly because Dartford was much nearer the realities of war and bombs. Despite the aerodromes and foreign troops in and around Stamford, German bombers somehow failed to find them.

Old friendships were revived, new alliances formed. With hormones stirring our social lives now included boys. There was a Youth Club in town but students from the 'posh' schools were not popular there and SHS staff preferred us to choose other ways to spend any spare time. We needed permission from school to go out in the evenings during the week, even with parents, though the same rule did not apply to Stamford School, apart from the boarders. We were rescued from boredom by Anne Halford's mother, who started 'The Young Players,' a club specialising in music and drama, to develop our interests in the Arts. We met in two rooms in Barn Hill Methodist Church where we would rehearse, give concerts and perform one-act plays to the general public, or simply parents and any friends who could be cajoled into supporting us. We also entered a few local Festivals.

Colin Dexter, later to become internationally famous as the creator of Inspector Morse, was Chairman. Even then he was a 'clever-clogs' with a brilliant wit, a seductive smile and a habit of spouting Latin or Greek in conversation, possibly to impress the girls. It worked, though I had eyes only for Bill Lack, my first big crush (not reciprocated.) Colin's older brother, John was passionate about classical music and together with Julian Aveling he organised the choir and musicians. I first sang Palestrina and Mozart's Ave Verum Corpus at The Young Players and I have nostalgic memories of playing table tennis with Bill. I wonder if we appreciated how fortunate we were.

I lied, though only a small lie, to get my first paid job. By quoting my Form number (Lower V, today's Year I0) I got away with being only thirteen rather than the legal fourteen. No one had time to check my honesty; there was a war on. The butcher on the corner at the top of Bentley Street paid me sixpence on Saturdays to struggle with a huge bike, with matching huge basket on the front, to deliver meat rations. The butcher's name was printed on a metal plate between the wheels, making it difficult to climb onto the saddle, which had to be lowered for me. I was handed a list of addresses, to be crossed out as each ticketed parcel was delivered. They were usually small packages, because the meat ration was pretty small, unless a family was huge or a close friend of the butcher. Surreptitious black market dealings with butchers, fishmongers and local farmers took place privately on weekdays, or so my mother said. I think she resented my not bringing home the odd spare joint. Stamford is almost as famed as Melton Mowbray for its pork butchers and our butcher made his own sausages. Sausages, like liver, kidneys, brains and the horrific sheep's head complete with eyes that Aunt Bess served up once, were not rationed. We regularly ate all of these, plus faggots. I'm not sure what went into the faggots and certainly never asked, as I was hungry enough not to complain. The sheep's head was different, it kept looking at me and I couldn't manage even a nibble. Together with brains, sweetbreads and tripe, no sheep's head has ever graced my table.

School became the main focus of my life. Not that I was a swot, but I was absorbing knowledge and attitudes which helped me escape, though not entirely, the grim life at home. We continued to live with the Great Aunts and as Gran had died, Mum and I now had a bedroom each, but I had so many chores. After school on most days, unless it was pouring with rain I had to go to the bowling green in the Recreation Ground. Aunt Bess was parked there by Mum or a neighbour for the afternoon and it was my job to push her home in her cumbersome wheelchair. A few minutes late and I'd be greeted by frowns and sulks.

There were two regular morning tasks before school, first carrying a white enamel pail upstairs and emptying chamber-pots from under Uncle Frank and Aunt Annie's bed, quite the worst job ever. Then downstairs I had to pull away the rug from the front door and stamp on any lurking beetle. Aunt Bess was beetle-phobic and the front room, her bedsit, opened directly onto the street. Her hideous pink metal false leg leaning against the bedpost scared me. She could walk only with two sticks and there were evenings when Mum and I would come home, perhaps from the cinema, to find her sitting in tears on the floor. She could drink a bottle of port wine in a couple of hours and if she dropped her sticks, with only one leg and the other badly scarred and in irons, she would fall and we had to lift her.
Having both Mum and Aunt Bess making demands was confusing. Mum found it difficult too and pretended she hadn't heard my question 'Mum, who do I have to obey? You and Aunt Bess tell me to do different things then you both get annoyed.'
It was hardly surprising that school provided a haven. Sweet Aunt Annie died early in 1945 and Uncle Frank took to his bed in an ever staler room. Fortunately in many ways, he lived on for only a few weeks. Mum fumigated the room, took over the double bed and I was released from slop pail duties.

The war was drawing to an obvious close. Soldiers from a nearby Prisoner of war camp were employed on local farms. Sylvia Storey's father was a farmer in Tinwell, a village a couple of miles outside Stamford. One Sunday evening Sylvia, Jean Atkin and I were picnicking with Mrs Storey by the river at the bottom of their fields. We were joined by three soldiers who asked politely in excellent English if they might sit down. Mrs Storey nodded and one of them began to play a harmonica. Any hostility we felt vanished as we were shown photos of wives and girl-friends, of Babies unseen for three years or more. Not the wicked Hun but ordinary young men only a few years older than us, with no more wish than our own soldiers to fight and to risk death. I had so much to think about – how could we so easily divide people into friend or foe, good or evil? A fourteen-year-old political animal was about to be born. Next day I saw one of the soldiers in the High Street. He greeted me but I was in school uniform and not allowed to speak to men at all. Embarrassed, I tried to explain quickly, but was unconvinced that he understood it was his gender and not his uniform I was avoiding.

In Europe millions of German troops had been captured, the campaign in Italy was over and British prisoners were no longer POWs (prisoners of war), which meant Uncle Bill would be coming home. On 30 April Hitler committed suicide with Eva Braun, who he'd married only a day or so earlier. We were excited and impatient, finding it difficult to concentrate in school – the teachers too - as we waited for peace to be declared.
On May 8th we assembled in the school hall just before 3 o'clock to hear the Prime Minister, Winston Churchill, announce
'Hostilities will end officially at one minute after midnight tonight, but in the interests of saving lives the 'Cease fire' began yesterday.'
We gave three cheers then were sent home for the two days' National holiday everyone had been eagerly awaiting.

Uncertainty about the actual date had allowed plenty of time to retrieve from cupboards and attics flags and bunting saved from before the war. Broad Street had been decorated for days and tables were now set up, loaded with food and drink, as much as we could eat, though we'd learned not to be greedy.
Most food had been rationed for years but for the Victory party the black market food which changed hands without coupons, often from local farmers, contributed vast plates of meat, fresh bread, creamy butter. The American GIs billeted in the district added far more from their regular food parcels and well-stocked canteen. Our usual party fare was fish paste or spam sandwiches and cakes made with dried egg, prunes and carrots. Today there was ham, beef, pies, American

candies. We'd grown used to doing without sweets and chewed until some of us felt sick. We drank synthetic fruit juice as there was no real lemonade. Like bananas, lemons were imported and I hardly remembered them; it would be some time before I saw one. The adults had plenty of beer.

Uncle Bill was home at last, he and his family had come to stay. We had all changed so much, I was no longer a nine-year-old and Uncle Bill was not the chirpy soldier I'd kissed goodbye. I hadn't seen him smile in the three days they'd been with us. My cousin John was four and a half; he wasn't born when his Dad left and hated this strange man arriving. He whined, misbehaved, kicked my Uncle on the shins and was slapped, hard. This was not the Uncle Bill I remembered. He'd been forced to march with hundreds of other prisoners across Poland, with shoes that wore out so they trod on bare stones, their feet cut to shreds. His legs became swollen, ulcerated and painful, never really healing. Uncle Bill walked very slowly like an old man, but he couldn't have been much over 30. I knew it would not be a good idea to mention that I'd talked to some German prisoners or describe their fairly easy lives working locally. I couldn't imagine Uncle Bill making my next birthday cake. He never again worked as a baker, if he worked at all.

No-one told us to go home, people danced and cheered until very late. It seemed only right to stay around our own families and I'm not sure the Ross family would have deigned to join the street party. Beth's father and her two brothers were still away, all three were RAF officers. Despite the aerodromes and the American and Polish Forces billeted locally, the war had seemed far away, but now the men would be coming home and no-one else would have to join up and go to fight. Some of the crowd went home early, many to mourn sons and husbands who would never return. Uncle Bill was neither dancing nor laughing.

The main difference I noticed in the days that followed was the lights everywhere. Blackout curtains were torn down, black paint and sticky tape scraped off windows, streetlights came on at dusk. Dad was still working at Vickers but no longer ferrying ammunition and he would soon be coming to live in Stamford with us. Ex-servicemen arrived home in shiny demob suits.

To prepare for the General Election, the school Discussion Group held a mock election. The results of its secret ballot, Liberals 38,

Conservatives 28, Labour 9 contradicted the general assumption that Mr Churchill would romp home as Prime Minister. A group of us went to hear a bald little man who we were told was Clement Attlee, the Labour Party leader. We very rudely laughed at his promises and scorned any idea of his becoming Prime Minister but the Labour Party landslide proved everyone wrong. Many of our teachers predicted that the commitment to nationalisation would lead to Soviet style government, warning that the school's status might be threatened. This latter did become an issue and the Governors chose to become independent, rather than a grammar school taking only pupils from Kesteven local authority. The latter would have meant that girls like me, from Kent, would have missed their opportunity.

In the last weeks of term, after the exams, V and VI formers worked to clear the 5000 sandbags still piled protectively round the outside walls, a tiring but satisfying job. While I was definitely a Tory, like my parents and most of the school, summer holidays loomed and I was interested less in politics than in plans for our eight-week break. There was still fighting in the Pacific but it didn't consciously affect me or my friends. School House boarders would be leaving for home and we could concentrate on the local lads and two-week, six-week, even six-month very chaste relationships.

The preaching of David Tryon from the South Africa General Mission attracted and I began reading my Bible every morning. Aunt Bess teased me horribly.

'Wait till he sits you on his knee. He's not Mr Try-it-on for nothing. Keep your legs crossed.'

The implication was false, but I stopped talking about Mr Tryon in front of her. The Mission held residential holidays in summer; I was offered a bursary and to my surprise was allowed to go.

During that week, on August 16th Japan capitulated and the final peace was declared. Three very distressed girls in my dormitory wept bitterly, refusing to join in the evening party, with its promise of hymn-singing and prayers of thanks. One was a Jewish refugee who had last seen her family being pushed onto a train by German soldiers, the others had fathers who had been killed in battle. I became even more confused about the war. No-one under sixteen had been allowed to see the first newsreels from Belsen. When I finally saw the newspaper photos and articles I understood why we'd had to fight. The images never faded. Our history syllabus had covered Tudors and Stuarts. It spoke of monasteries destroyed, a fire from 'Pudding Lane to Pie Corner,' unfaithful kings and a virgin queen. And Shakespeare.

In the first week of the new term the Upper school went to Peterborough to see the film of Laurence Olivier in 'Henry V.' Local schools were invited at least once a year to special free matinees in the Stamford cinema. Miss Tebbs, one of our English teachers summarised the play before we went, analysing some of the speeches. It has always been my favourite Shakespeare play, despite Miss Tebbs' teasing,

'Maggie – short for magpie, which means "Chatterbox.'

She was staring straight at me, but I enjoyed her sense of humour. I soon had reason to be grateful to her.

Our form mistress reminded us next day that we must concentrate on working for the Oxford School Certificate Exams next summer. Most people took seven subjects, with eight for the more academic among us. My least favourite subject was biology, but a science was compulsory; I wasn't good at chemistry and had never learned physics. The teacher, Miss Rigby, rather obviously known as Riggles was both boring and squeamish. For reproduction we examined a dissected rabbit, the lesson ending with

'Humans do that too.'

'Ugh!' was our united response.

It is possible that Riggles understood child psychology. I had more than one detention for talking in class and she informed me on one of these occasions

'You're bright under all your silliness. It's a pity you're going to fail.'

Oh no, I wasn't. I would do enough work to pass if only to prove the stupid woman wrong.

Beth was still my best friend, but she was in Lower V and under less pressure. Homework began to take priority, we would go out on Saturdays, but weekday evenings were sacrosanct, I wasn't going to give Dad any reason to say the school had been a waste of time and I really enjoyed most of the work.

The exams were graded Distinction; Credit; Pass and Fail. I managed four Distinctions and four Credits, including biology. Riggles offered a knowing smirk as she congratulated me on my Credit. That year I gained my first school prize 'For good work in the Oxford School Certificate Examinations' and chose the Complete Shakespeare. No congratulations from Dad, he simply said

'About time you brought a prize home. Don't understand a ruddy word of the book, though.'

Post-war school magazines

With School Cert. out of the way, to my horror my parents spent the last three weeks of term hinting that I should think about leaving school and getting a job. Mum wrote to the Head and both parents were invited to see her, but as Dad was not yet living with us Mum had a cast iron excuse for his absence. That weekend she told Dad 'She'll have to stay on for one term, we forgot to give notice. The school want her to stay on and go to University. She's a clever kid, you know.'

His response?

'Waste of time, she'll only get married. That school's cost more than enough.'

This was not strictly true, the scholarship and uniform grant covered most of the expenses and clothes rationing ensured I had few non-school outfits, but he may have had in mind my lack of contribution to the household.

'Why can't she learn typing at evening classes?'

Miss Tebbs called me back one afternoon as I was packing my satchel to go home. Tebbs was very direct, critical but never cruel.

'Are you rushing off somewhere? I'd like a word.'

Somehow it didn't sound like a telling-off.

'I'll catch you up' I said to my grinning friends.

'Don't hover there looking bewildered, doesn't suit you. What's this I hear about you leaving at the end of term? Are you completely mad or is there another reason?'

'My parents don't think it's worth staying on. They want me to learn shorthand and typing.'

'*They* want it or are you after an early pay packet?'

I was embarrassed. Tebbs was waiting for a reply.

'My Dad doesn't agree with girls being educated, he says I'll only get married.'

'Hrrumph. Send him to see me.'

I wasn't sure who'd come off worse and was snob enough not to want them to meet.

'He's not here all the time.'

'Still in the Forces?'

'He was medically unfit. He drove an ammunition lorry.'

'You're one of my bright hopes. Far too few women get to University. It would be criminal to stop you at this stage. You'd get a good grant. Try to talk him round.'

She'd never met my father. And never would, he avoided ever crossing the threshold of Stamford High. Miss Tebbs finally seemed to grasp from my silence that the enemy was more him than Mum. It took years for me to see that *his* enemy was social class – and intelligent women.

I told Mum what Miss Tebbs had said and begged her not to make me leave. Mum was still working at Blackstone's and had early notice of any vacancies, so she soon found Dad a job there. I wasn't sure I enjoyed having him around all the time, he was so critical of me, but he accepted grudgingly that I must spend at least a term in the sixth form, so I went back and chose my subjects for Higher School Certificate, the last one before the introduction of A-Levels. I continued with the ones where I'd gained Distinctions in School Cert. English, French and History with Geography as a subsidiary. Would I be there long enough to take them? If not, what then?

A TEMPORARY REPRIEVE

On an obvious path to university? My parents' views had not altered since my conversation with Miss Tebbs. Staying on for Lower VI was a hard-won but fruitful concession. I'm among those whose schooldays, certainly at Stamford, were some of the best years of their lives. I began to broaden my interests and to shoulder, pretty lightly, more responsibilities. I was in the school choir, chaired the Debating Society, became House Captain, a Sub-prefect , a Prefect and played Mr Hardcastle to Beth's Kate in 'She Stoops to Conquer.'.

She Stoops to Conquer

The VI form years were punctuated by boyfriends, brief or occasionally semi-serious relationships. They were mainly with boys from School House; rule-breaking making them more glamorous. Dick Buckley was the sender of my most treasured Valentine, printed indelibly on my memory alongside the long-abandoned Lord's Prayer.
'My figure may not be so fine, my face may not be thrilling,
But if you want a Valentine, I'm very weak and willing.'
Could a sixteen-year-old ask more? Dick would risk the two of us being caught in one of the school music rooms in the evenings, serenading me on a grand piano with 'The Dream of Olwen.' A great romantic, shyly humorous, he once chided me for my lack of

pavement manners, grinning as he said
'If you were a lady you'd walk on the inside.'
A regular visitor at home, he often polished my shoes.
'My dad told me if you love a woman you'll clean her shoes for her,'
he said, the first time he did so.
Dick's father had been a professional footballer, before the war,
playing for Doncaster Rovers and was now the landlord of a
Doncaster pub, 'The Blue Bell.' Dick took me to meet them and I was
made very welcome. Not all public schoolboys are from the middle or
upper classes and maybe our similar backgrounds drew us together.
Being a scholarship girl at Stamford High included enduring painful
moments of snobbish nose-tilting.

Young love - with Dick 1947

I'm not sure why the relationship ended, probably because Dick left
school a year before me and at 17 I was fickle. It was barely three
years since war had taught our older sisters how fragile relationships
could be. Many of their boyfriends, fighter pilots and gunners from the
local aerodromes, were killed in action. Once they left school our
young men too would face compulsory National Service, though now
with less risk of being killed or taken prisoner.

In November 1946 the whole Upper School spent an afternoon at the
cinema, watching 'Theirs Is the Glory,' a documentary about the
British 1st Airborne Division's part in the battle of the Dutch city of
Arnhem. All the actors were serving soldiers, mainly parachutists,
demonstrating genuine heroism rather than Hollywood versions.
Propaganda to persuade young people that the war had been worth
it? VI-formers later saw a film of the bombing of Hiroshima, which was
responsible, or so we'd been led to believe, for ending the war in the
East. Loud applause greeted the end of the film, countered back at
school by impassioned arguments from both teachers and students

.

over the ethics of unleashing the horrors, as we had soon discovered, of atomic warfare.

At Christmas, together with several of my friends I became a temporary Christmas postman. This time the white lie was unnecessary as it was taken for granted that we were all 16, the legal minimum age. The war and the danger of our being captured or the mail stolen by spies safely over, we battled with heavy sacks, frequently saturated by rain or snow. There was the awful day, gloves soaked and hands freezing, when by mistake I dropped cards for several addresses into one large letterbox. I knocked at the door, was given a grudging 'Christmas Box' and a warning not to try that trick too often, my embarrassment and abject apology ignored.

The Headmistress made a disastrous announcement in the last Assembly of term. Miss Tebbs was moving to Tasmania and would be leaving at Easter. I was relying on her support in any further argument with my parents about my future. Dad was already talking about giving in my notice so I would leave in summer. I spent the Christmas holidays on my best behaviour, anxious about Dad's stubbornness. Maybe Mum's influence, strengthened by memories of her own unappreciated intelligence when she was at school, changed his mind. He decided
'You may as well take the blasted exams but then you'll definitely have to get a job.'
He grudgingly accepted the hug I gave him but Mum was thrilled when I hugged her in turn. Physical affection was rare in our household.

From late January until March England was buried, almost literally in places, in the worst winter so far of the 20th century, with February the coldest ever recorded. Coal trains could not reach power stations, many towns and main roads were cut off for weeks. With coal in very short supply our house was often freezing. I would wake shivering, the windows obscured not by blackouts but by intricate designs of frost and ice on the inside. I had dreadful chilblains and had to take time off school, as neither my own shoes nor Mum's, two sizes larger, would fit my swollen and painful feet. An embarrassing but acceptable excuse; it would have been unreasonable to spend precious clothing coupons on temporary shoes.
On the last day of term I went to see Miss Tebbs.
'It's goodbye, then. Any news on the University front?'
she asked.

'No. I wish you weren't leaving. At least he's letting me stay next year but then he says I've got to start work.'
'Exams are a start, you never know. Whatever happens, don't ever stop asking questions or reading and if you get the chance, take it. It's been a joy, most of the time, to teach you.'
She smiled, I blinked, several times.
'Let's not be sentimental. Off you go.'

With spring came exciting developments in the world of fashion. As teenagers our appearance was a major priority and we were more than ready to move away from utility and second-hand clothes. Christian Dior launched what Harper's Bazaar's editor, Carmel Snow, called 'Such a new look!'
It heralded full calf-length skirts, wasp waists, yards and yards of fabric, a refreshing change. Any clothes we bought now must follow Dior's New Look. Beth was first to sport a long skirt, I had to wait until it was time for a new winter coat, though I made myself a summer skirt, a poor copy but it felt like high fashion.

Beth and I were allowed to go on our first holiday without adults. We went by train, the worn and scruffy seats not particularly comfortable as no-one had yet invested in new stock, but at least we could sit down. Wartime trains had been packed with army, navy and air force personnel, with standing room only. People were asked to stay put where possible and I'd rarely been on a train during the war. We went to Hoo in Kent, a name good for a giggle, to stay with Bob and Ivy Vidgeon, fruit farmers Dad had met early in the war, when he worked on the site of a new army camp next to their farm. Our parents assumed we'd be safe under the chaperonage of Auntie Ivy, but she had no children and thought young girls should have fun. We went to village dances, flirted with the local boys, made lifelong enemies of the girls, were kissed on haystacks, came home late but sober, grew up a little.

September brought Upper VI and a prefect's badge. Upper VI meant working hard for exams, but not before a national holiday in November 1947 for the wedding of Princess Elizabeth and Philip, her 'handsome Greek sailor.' (Daily Mail). Six of us, Beth, Monica and me with our School House - and therefore officially forbidden - boyfriends went to Uppingham to sample the delights of a hotel meal, naively overlooking the possibility that parents of other boarders might do the same. We spent an embarrassing hour subjected to the sniggering of younger boys who recognised in Dick, Bob Pearce and Barry Beardall three of their fellow boarders, all VI-formers. Fortunately none seemed to sneak, or if they did we heard nothing more.

There was another narrow escape at Christmas, when we met for mince pies and a quick kiss'n'cuddle in the boys' Sports pavilion before the joint schools Carol Concert at Stamford School. How were we to know that one of the staff would be walking his dog on the playing field? Our whispers set the animal barking. We clambered out through a back window, scrambled up the bank and lay in quivering heaps as the hound sniffed our trail. There was a full moon and I'm certain we were seen, but the teacher was a good sport and still young himself. I almost left my hat behind, Cash's name tape and all which would have done for us, but Dick picked it up, handed it to me and I slunk into the back row of the choir as the lights lowered. We heard nothing more, though Monty's younger brother Keith was quizzed about a bag of buns found in the pavilion marked 'Hudson, Monday.' Fortunately he had an alibi – and an innocent smile.

Unlike the Sunday in spring when Mrs Deed, wife of Stamford School's Headmaster, came across Monica and Barry in the woods. Dick and I were another of the couples lurking behind trees. Not *in flagrante*, we were all far too innocent, but even an arm round the waist was a serious crime; these vulnerable young males needed protecting from predatory young women. We all 'fessed up' and were duly humiliated, being sent one by one to apologise to the Head of the other school, giving us heroic status among our peers. Mr Deed said little beyond
'I trust such an event will never occur again.'
I suspect Miss Lomax was more amused than angry.
Miss Richardson, my pompous Form mistress told me to resign my prefect-ship. I went to see the Head.
'Miss Richardson told me to report to you. She thinks I have disgraced the school and should give up my Prefect's badge.'
'And what do you think? Do you not value the role – or this school?'
'Of course I do. Resigning wasn't my idea.'
If I sounded sulky it was because tears were lurking.
'No need for such drastic action. Be more discreet in future, rules are there for a reason. This incident is now closed.'
There was a definite twinkle in her eye. We made sure we weren't caught again, which Miss Lomax was possibly hinting.

I enjoyed games and gym, sporting both a blue Gymnastics and a red Deportment stripe on the V of my school tunic. Good carriage was essential, one of the Prefects' tasks was patrolling the corridors between lessons, urging girls to take their satchels off their shoulders and stand up straight. I captained my House at hockey, played both in the First XI and the County XI trials and have a permanently swollen ankle to prove it, from being continually hit by a hard hockey ball. Was this keenness an effort to please Dad? None of my friends looked forward to games, or gym lessons!

STAMFORD HIGH SCHOOL

1ST XI. HOCKEY, 1948-1949

Tennis was less successful, I never made even the second team. One of our more famous pupils, Margaret Emerson, then Vice-Captain of the Junior Lawn Tennis Club of Great Britain, was a boarder in my year. I played opposite her once, with a humiliating and brief 6-0, 6-0 score. Boarders could use the school courts at weekends and Margaret would often be in the playground as we arrived on weekday mornings, slamming a ball against a wall. Day girls were limited to the town courts, which were often fully booked, with priority given to ex-armed forces. In these early post-war years racquets and balls were of poor quality and pretty scarce, but we'd known nothing else and enjoyed a few sets at weekends and in the holidays.

Prefects were privileged to give detentions, presumably intended to encourage us in making mature decisions, for less serious rule-breaking like running in the corridors. We may have abused it a little. Sitting in the Library after school listening to juniors reciting Wordsworth's 'On Westminster Bridge' probably gave more girls a hatred of poetry than an appreciation of Wordsworth. My least favourite Romantic poet, he was one of the four I had to study for English and I confess rather viciously enjoyed their bored recitals.

The Debating Society was stimulating and I was often the proposer or opponent of the subject, including
'That the present system of advertising is pernicious,'
which was defeated by a large majority. As the media was limited mainly to the press, magazines, billposting or the odd commercial radio station ('We are the Ovaltineys' was a regular weekly treat on Radio Luxembourg before the war) I can't vouch for the nature of the perniciousness.
I would prefer to forget my most famous victory, by 22 votes to 13, when I proposed that
'A woman cannot successfully combine a career and marriage.'
My opinions at the time must have been influenced by my own experience of a mother who I'd always felt preferred work to her daughter. The report in the school magazine includes the comment
'If both husband and wife had a career the husband should give substantial help to his wife with the housework. Possibly owing to the fact that the male point of view was not represented, the suggestion met with unanimous approval.'

Miss Lomax and before her Miss Nicol firmly believed in developing women's intellects. I spent a weekend as part of the school team at a British Commonwealth Youth Conference and another at the Annual Youth Conference at Peterborough. Our cultural lives were important too, there were regular concerts at both schools with musicians like Dennis Brain and of course Sir Malcolm Sargent, himself a Stamfordian. We were taken to London to see Laurence Olivier in 'King Lear,' combining it with a visit to the Royal Academy. Three of us escaped to the preferred delights of the food emporium in Fortnum & Mason, followed during our 'tour' at a less than discreet distance by uniformed security guards, girls in school uniform offering more a warning than a guarantee of honesty.

In the final terms of Upper VI concentration on exams was paramount. Although the majority of leavers went to teacher training colleges or into nursing, this was more a reflection of contemporary society than the school's ambitions. All the teachers' attempts to persuade my parents to let me go to university emphasised their determination to improve women's possible options, but there was no point in applying. Even if Dad showed signs of weakening, I would have had to wait a further year, but I was determined to work for good results.

THE FUTURE BECKONS

Winning a scholarship when I was still only ten caught up with me after Higher School Certificate exams were over. University applicants had to be eighteen in the November before entry, regardless of exam results, so I was not eligible for another year. This made it easier than ever for my father to deride the 'waste of time' and I tended to agree with him on that point. I suspect Miss Lomax still hoped to convert my parents. As the Civil Service exams would be in spring 1949 she convinced them it made sense to stay on at school and prepare for them, to ensure a good grade.

Third-year VI was a great year, there were only five of us and we were each offered a choice of courses, often with a teacher to ourselves. I picked up the German I'd begun at Dartford, explored demography with Miss Gregory and three of us joined the current Upper VI English A-level group, whose set books were different from the previous year. They envied our freedom from exam pressure.

My appointment as Vice-head of school was, said my friends, very appropriate. Vice, before I undertook this responsible role, had been limited to such daring adventures as walking out of Miss Marshall's English lessons early, pretending we were 'country girls' with a bus to catch. Poor Miss Marshall – Granny Honk to us - was well past retirement age but came for two terms as a supply teacher. We treated her appallingly, but it was she who made Shakespeare's Richard 11 come alive with her explanations of Richard's dilemmas and emphasis on the language, she who introduced me to the poet Francis Thompson. Religion was now far less prominent in my life, but the lyricism and mysticism of 'Oh, world invisible, we view thee' and the yearnings of 'The Hound of Heaven' moved me and have remained in my memory as few other religious poets have.
We had to skulk in nearby Burghley Park in case we were seen in our uniforms before the school day ended, but at least we'd rebelled. If only I could have carried that rebellious spirit home.

Slightly more reprehensible sins included meeting boys, sometimes in coffee houses after dark. This was not expressly forbidden us, sixth-formers were allowed out until 9p.m. without permission, but the boys were boarders, with girls and evening outings definitely off limits.

57

Being Vice Head girl made no difference to these adventures but we were careful not to be caught!

The theme of the annual local Youth Conference was exploring working conditions and our team was charged with visiting the local hospital. This was fascinating, as it was a year since the National Health Service was introduced. We were becoming adults, involved in the citizenship Miss Lomax taught the VI Form. Here we'd learned how Parliament functioned, how newspapers were produced, had spent several lessons debating the Beveridge Report. This declared that there were 'five giants' to be slain during post-war reconstruction: want, disease, squalor, ignorance and idleness. Interviewing staff at the Infirmary gave us an opportunity to explore how disease and working conditions were being tackled.

School provided leisure activities which encouraged our social skills. The VI Form held an annual Christmas party for the Upper IIIs (Year 7); we were invited to a heavily supervised party at Stamford School, no couples in corners or outside the hall, and we gave the staff a party. Here I reached the finals of the table-tennis tournament, my opponent the Head! Miss Lomax won, though I can't claim that I deliberately allowed her victory.

Several teachers expressed sadness that I'd chosen not to go to University.
Chosen? Sadness was not my main emotion, I was more bitter than sad. I'd been winning Form Prizes, my exam results were similar to Margaret Wyman's who was going next year to London University, and better than most of the others who were now in some form of further education. My parents saw the Civil Service as the acme of achievement and there was no way I could find the courage, or the arguments, to defy them.

I was unaware for many years how threatened Dad must have felt by these women of his. A clever wife made to leave school at 14 and apprenticed to a milliner even though she hated sewing. Who after a few months, without telling her termagant of a mother found herself an office job and ended up in 1929 as manager of a Marks and Spencer's Penny Bazaar. Dad left school at 12, barely literate with few aspirations beyond manual labour and keeping in work. Now he had a daughter who might be even brighter than his wife. Between us we must have made him feel totally inadequate, but at seventeen I simply felt defeated and resentful.

In March 1949 Pat McCarthy, Hazel Porter and I went to London to sit the Executive Civil Service Exam. Four days off school, all expenses paid. I stayed with Uncle Charles and Auntie Rosie who now lived in a newly-built bungalow in Woking, a sign that they had moved much further up the status ladder than the rest of the family. Uncle Charles met me at Waterloo station every evening, so there were no wild parties, nor even clandestine friendships. We did the school proud, which only served to confirm Miss Lomax's despair. Out of 1857 entrants Pat came 9th, with 100% and 95% for maths; I was 83rd, with 86% for Literature and a distinction in compulsory English. There was a compulsory maths paper too, probably to ensure we spent our monthly pay cheque wisely, but my marks there were nothing to boast about.

Next step the interview. Clothes rationing had ended a few weeks earlier so I invested my savings in a lavender blue costume (suit, in today's language), the jacket with a nipped-in waist, the skirt flared and calf-length. Dior's New Look, but rather less expensive. I already had a blouse in fashionable 'dusky pink' and my shoes and gloves were respectable. The final touch was a pink bowler hat; like the gloves, a hat was essential, but I suspect I never wore it again. My interview was at noon so I could travel from Stamford and back in one day, alone as in 1939, but by train and unchaperoned this time, with a travel voucher and map of London. It was the first modern map I'd seen. No street maps had been issued to the public during the war as they might help the enemy to reach Downing Street, or possibly Harrods.

An intrepid explorer, I caught a 77 bus from Kings Cross to Whitehall, but failed to discover the designated Government department. Pacing up and down past Horse Guards Parade I was far too nervous to eye up the soldiers. I finally found the building, The Treasury, to be greeted kindly by a doorman wearing the black jacket with brass crown buttons that would become so familiar.

'Interview, dear? Upstairs, turn right, you'll see the others waiting. Good luck.'

If I were successful would I still be 'Dear' or would it be 'Miss Fairman' or possibly even 'Madam'? Youth is so arrogant.

Three others were perched on a bench next to a door marked 'Interview in Progress' and we exchanged brief grimaces. My name was called and I entered the interview room. Should I keep my hat on? Where to put my gloves? I screwed these into a ball on my lap, attempting to conceal how intimidating I found the four people seated at the table. Some of the questions seemed irrelevant; my defiance of authority (outside the home) was already entrenched.

'What does your father do?'

Why? He wasn't after the job, I was. Should I answer 'Shout at me and Mum, go to the pub, drive a lorry?'

Possibly not.

'He works for Blackstone's, agricultural engineers.'

'Uh-huh.'

They knew this, the details were in front of them.

'I see you want to join the Foreign Office. What books would you take with you to a strange country?'

I'd grown up through a war. Apart from newsreels I'd watched of Germany, Holland, France, Japan and America, plus films portraying their own versions of local life, all countries outside England were strange. What impression did I want to give?

'Shakespeare, Tolstoy, T S Eliot.'

Classics and a poet, a contemporary literary star. I'd show them I how earnest I was.

'Wouldn't you take a dictionary?'

Ouch. Get out of that one.

'I took it for granted that I'd be provided with one.'

Cheeky? That remark, plus my father's lowly status, may have convinced them I wasn't diplomatic material. The Foreign Office was closed to me and with hindsight we would have had little in common, but I did get the Colonial Office. A consolation prize?

Library books told me about the colonies, how many, where they were, how wonderfully we governed them. Africa was not exactly the Brazilian post I coveted, but I never managed to visit any colony.

I was preparing to make the most of my final term at SHS until a cinema visit soon after Easter, where streptococci had invaded, attacking with triumphal cries the blood of convenient victims, or so the doctors told me. Two nights later I woke around 3a.m. clutching damp sheets, a fire burning my throat. The damp was sweat, my throat so swollen I could hardly speak and I was diagnosed with scarlet fever. Mum was offered the option of an isolation hospital some miles away, or keeping me at home with sheets over the bedroom door to prevent infection, delicate diets, chamber pots to empty until I was well enough to go downstairs to the outside toilet. Not a situation to be tolerated by Mum, nursing never a favoured occupation. Her trump card:

'Your friends will come round and I'll have a job keeping them out.'

Antibiotics had not yet reduced scarlet fever to a mere 'streptococcal infection' and I was sent packing to the Isolation hospital in Peterborough. Each illness was in a separate ward - three whooping cough cases kept each other company while I languished alone, frequently full of weeping self-pity. Close family were allowed weekly visits, but were forced to stand outside, speaking into a barely open window, hardly cheery sessions. Conversing at bedsides is awkward at the best of times and Dad's jokes now were even less intelligible than his usual efforts.

There was one advantage. As the only patient in the ward I had sole charge of the radio. I listened non-stop to the Home Service, forerunner of Radio 4 and was particularly enchanted by an evening series introducing opera for beginners. I heard excerpts from Carmen, Tosca, La Bohème and others and knew that one day I would make sure I saw and heard this marvellous music onstage. My first visit to an opera house had to wait another seven years. I had enjoyed school concerts and musicians' recitals, and had a small part in the joint schools production of 'Dido and Aeneas.' Classical music and opera were added to theatre and film as major loves, though at home there was no encouragement to listen to 'that rubbish.'

There were two regular nurses, one of them male. Unfit for active service he had chosen to nurse, and stayed on after the war. He was delightful company and would stay to chat whenever he found me weeping. The other nurse's Irish brogue kept me wide-eyed with tales of her obsessively jealous boyfriend. I hope she left him. The war had been over for four years but most food was still rationed. Friends and neighbours showed their sympathy by sacrificing their sweet rations, bagsful would arrive on Saturdays with Mum and Dad and I went home three weeks later almost a stone heavier.

I was still considered infectious, so spent another fortnight sunning myself in the back yard. John Clark, my current boyfriend, another boarder, sent postcards, but our romance was squashed by his fear of contagion – he *was* going to be a medical student!
A mere half term was left when I returned to school, quite the suntanned heroine, though there were disadvantages. No tennis, no swimming, no running, horrific peeling of skin from legs and arms.
In the last week of term the Prize List was read out. I was unlikely to hear my name, as third-year VI meant no exams and I was not going on to higher education. I'd forgotten the Teasdale Prize, first awarded two years earlier to Mary Teasdale. A heroine of mine, Mary was

funny, had played Noah in the school play, captained the first XI and was a great role model. I half-listened to the Head's words.

'The Teasdale Prize for the inspiration and encouragement of others goes to Margaret Fairman. The prize is awarded both for creativity outside the curriculum and for services to the school.'

My most treasured prize

I'd had a major part in 'She Stoops to Conquer', was House Captain, Deputy Head girl, a first XI hockey player. But I'd also, in Lower VI, heard my name read aloud in the hall for 'letting down the school' by misbehaving (giggling very loudly with friends) at a concert, plus the Sunday Wothorpe Woods episode, both times with the forbidden word 'boys' involved. No-one could have appreciated this prize more than I. Inspiring and encouraging others became, unconsciously, a mantra for my proper career. My family considered it nothing special; but then they saw little in me that was special. I wasn't a boy.

Last day of term. Tears as we sang 'Within These Walls of Grey' at our final Assembly, more tears plus small gifts from younger girls with 'crushes' on Prefects. So many people I would miss, teachers, friends scattering to college, some not yet leaving, like Beryl Mawer who had become a close friend. A final look round the VI form room then drifting slowly, with my cronies, into the playground and through the gate. Time to go. Sticking to tradition, we marched down the hill to the bridge, threw our hats into the River Welland, cheering as they disappeared, to resurface for a while in the Meadows. I wonder if this is still a custom; doubt it, doubt if hats are worn today. I kept my hatband and badge for years and still have my Prefect badge.

LONDON HERE I COME

W hile I waited for the letter demanding my presence in London, I spent a few weeks as a temporary teacher at St Martin's Junior Boys School. Qualifications were not then essential and I had no idea how to teach them anything, certainly no way of keeping small boys quiet. One morning I told a group of chatterboxes to stay behind after school and was met with tears. At lunchtime the Headmaster sent for me and explained kindly that I was not allowed to give detentions without consulting a 'real' teacher. These boys were Barnardo's orphans and would be in trouble if they were late home or reported as badly behaved. Not quite Dotheboys Hall, but visions of bowls of gruel left me feeling quite motherly. Grateful for the 'pardon,' the boys were angelic for the rest of my stay, but the experience confirmed that teaching small children was no profession for me.

A week after I left St Martin's with a very diplomatic letter of recommendation, for my attitude and reliability rather than teaching skills, came the day to leave home. Dad was casual as ever. A brief peck on the cheek, an admonition to behave myself and he was off to work. Mum was distant too, but more from umbrage. It hadn't occurred to me she would expect to come with me, to confirm that I would not be living in some den of iniquity.
'I'm a big girl now, Mum, it's not school. Come for a weekend when I'm settled,'
had heralded three days of silence and heavy dusting. Her father's suicide had left a legacy of feelings unexpressed or denied, silence her only weapon. A habit I inherited.

Was I anxious? I was certainly excited, I was about to live in London, earning a monthly salary. No-one in our family, with the possible exception of Mum's brother Charles, had ever known anything but a weekly wage in a brown pay-packet, although as office staff at Blackstone's Mum was entitled to a white envelope. I'm sure neither of my parents had a bank account, until in 1952 Mum worked for United Dominions Trust when she too received a monthly salary cheque.

The Colonial Office Welfare Officer had sent me a travel voucher and another map, this time of the London Underground. I eventually found my way to Holland Park to meet her at the imposing Georgian villa now converted into a women's hostel. She left after introducing me to the Warden, who gave me a key accompanied by a lecture on curfews (10 o'clock unless with express permission) and male visitors, strictly sitting-room only and never overnight, even brothers. She showed me the dining room and the bathrooms, then took me up to where I would be living, a dormitory shared with five others. I wondered where I would put any smuggled overnight male.

Room-mates included Mona, a Polish refugee who cried every evening for the husband and daughter back home; Carol, an actress I saw years later on TV in Upstairs Downstairs and my best friend there, Eirlys of the soft Welsh accent. Eirlys and I went fairly regularly to Methodist services at Central Hall Westminster, to the theatre, normally in the 'Gods' and once to see the great Leonide Massine dance. My home was now a bed, a bedside table and a wardrobe, none with locks. Moving to Holland Park coincided with a lingering religious ambivalence, so my bedside table housed a Bible which I read every morning and an unabridged copy of 'Lady Chatterley's Lover' in a brown paper cover, for bedtime guilty reading. Prayers including 'Forgive us our trespasses' justified this suspect reading life.

It took some weeks to work out the connection between Trafalgar Square, Oxford Circus and Marble Arch, but the Tube was no problem as long as I stuck to the District and Circle lines which sped me to work, to Sloane Square (Jo), South Kensington (Beth), Notting Hill for cinema and coffee bars, the Strand for Lyons Corner House and theatres. My salary left enough spare cash for occasional shopping. Clothes rationing had ended a few months before I left school, no more make-do-and-mend. I could buy what I wanted or could afford, although there were still many shortages. Before I left Stamford I'd spent the money I'd earned from teaching on a few items suitable for my new status. My Interview suit was fine for work, but I needed an occasional change of outfit. I limited myself to a couple of skirts and jumpers (not yet graced by the American 'sweater') and a dressing gown for modesty. Stamford was not exactly a fashion centre, but fashion was waiting in Oxford Street department stores.

Weekends were for exploring a London which after life in a small market town was highly glamorous. My social life expanded. Jo, now a third-year nurse at Tite Street Children's Hospital in Chelsea, introduced me to dishy medical students, Beth was at the Webber Douglas School of Dramatic Art, her fellow students including Michael Bryant and others who would become recognised. Drama school parties offered this naïve country bumpkin a few shocking revelations. Grabbing my coat from a bed when I went home I might interrupt drunken groping, contacting a bare leg, or worse. Then there was the first time I saw two men kissing. Homosexuality was illegal and while, despite all the adverse propaganda I was not bothered that some of her fellow students were gay, I'd never thought about the physical side of this and was startled.

'Don't tell a soul' warned Beth, 'They could be arrested.'

From Monday 16th October 1949 I became officially an Executive officer in the Colonial Office, based for my six weeks' induction in the two main buildings in Great Smith Street, then allocated to a more permanent post in Social Services Department in Victoria Street. I was instructed to open a bank account as my salary would be paid in monthly. Barclays in Horseferry Road, Westminster was the nearest. It would be almost three years before I became officially an adult, but according to Dad I'd joined the 'nobs.'

Two smart civil servants. With Margaret Fairlie

Early in 1950 Mum and Dad saw a notice in a newspaper that a solicitor was searching for George Fairman. They were nervous, but Dad was not wanted for any crime, they were tracing him as a householder. I have no idea why, but they had never claimed back the Gipsy Road house. With the papers signed Dad came back to live in London, where he soon found a job. I was expected to join him as housekeeper (not that anyone phrased it in those words) while he redecorated the whole house for Mum's return.

We spent a few weeks tolerating each other. I was earning my living and contributing but he was uneasy with my friends. The effects on family life of upward mobility can be long-lasting and are insufficiently recorded. I resented leaving Holland Park but I was still under age and had little alternative. I did basic, very basic, cooking and housework; helping Dad with wallpapering and paint offered common ground.

'Not a bad effort, we'll make a tradesman of you yet,'
was high praise and perhaps revealed his longing for a son he could understand and who might respect him.

The education issue never went away. Mary Darlow, my first boss was totally unable to comprehend my parents' attitude. Terrifying, brilliantly intellectual, public school and Oxford educated, her pores oozed class background. I'd been to a public school too, but only because of the war and a scholarship. I tried to explain.

'My parents thought I'd been educated long enough to earn a living. And I'm only a girl.'

'A bit exaggerated.' Darlow's favourite phrase. 'Think again, my girl. You have as much right as any man to a University education.'

Not women with fathers like mine, but there was no point in continuing the discussion.

Two of the Advisers in my Department were helpful.

'If University is out of the question, why not teach? Homerton is the finest teacher training college in the country and has the advantage of being in Cambridge.'

This was Freda Gwilliam, Education Adviser, more empathic than Miss Darlow but equally determined I would move on. Homerton College offered me an interview and then a place, but as usual I allowed my parents to talk me out of it, though I may also have had at the back of my mind St Martin's School and my vow never to become a teacher.

Back to the idea of a degree. Mr Chinn, Miss Gwilliam's colleague, suggested the London School of Economics. As a late entrant I was required to submit an essay entitled 'Higher Education – Vocational or Intellectual?' My somewhat muddled arguments must have either impressed or intrigued them and I began a part-time degree, never completed, the complex entry requirements partly responsible. I had excellent exam results but no Latin A- level, although I did have Matriculation exemption, an essential then, so I was syphoned into Economics, with Psychology, my first choice, as a subsidiary subject.

An understanding of economics and more especially of statistics eluded me. After we were shown old exam papers whose questions

66

may as well have been in Greek, I developed symptoms of an ulcer and left after two terms. I loved the other lectures, especially history and sociology, a relatively new subject. I also met a witty Bernard Levin who was in his final year and gained a boyfriend, Gordon. A red-headed devout Methodist, he invited me to church then home to tea and hymn-singing with his parents. Not entirely my style, though his parents were delightful. We took my parents to the theatre, a very rare outing for Dad. Gordon's rudeness during the interval finished that relationship as he replied in response to Dad's
'Beer then, lad?'
'I don't approve of people who drink alcohol.'

I became resigned to remaining a civil servant. The uncarpeted stairs of our office in Victoria Street reverberated from a constant stream of dejected and angry Jamaicans who had been arriving since 1948 on the Empire Windrush, enticed by stories of jobs and riches, now anxious to blame the Colonial Office for broken promises. Part of my job was to arrange tours for colonial staff visiting Britain to research public service provision. I met my first black professionals, mainly from the West Indies, often with a delicious sense of humour about white people's ill-concealed reactions to their skin colour.

Staff in the South Africa section taught me about the disgrace that was apartheid.
'Notice,' they said, 'that it is pronounced 'apart-hate.'
Another political wake-up call. Stamford High had hardly nurtured left-wing values. These were important years, though I'm not sure I appreciated my good fortune in working with people involved in events like the partition of Palestine, begun in 1948 but certainly not settled; the Tanganyika groundnuts scandal, South African troubles and later, in my next posting, Archbishop Makarios and Enosis in Cyprus, Ian Smith in Rhodesia, Mau Mau in Kenya.

Work offered ample leisure opportunities. I joined the Colonial Office choir; its conductor, Robert Armstrong (now Lord Armstrong) of the Treasury, became famous for the phrase 'economical with the truth' during the 'Spycatcher' trial in 1986. We sang in St Stephens' Chapel at the Houses of Parliament and at a Mozart 200th Anniversary concert where the soloist was April Cantelo, at that time Robert Armstrong's wife. I was mixing, however marginally, with the famous.

A lesser status was offered by the Colonial Office Drama Society. More interesting productions came later from membership of the

Festival Players in Catford, after Eric Weedon, a C.O. Drama Society member, introduced me. My favourite role was Celia in 'As You Like It,' a production with a few simple props which we took on tour to small halls, gardens, local children's homes and a hospice. Other productions were The Rivals and The Cherry Orchard, but my greatest hour came with a glowing review in the local paper of 'She Stoops to Conquer,' where I played Kate this time.

'For Goldsmith she stooped to conquer, for her Lewisham audience she reached high,'

might have led to my becoming the first Dame Maggie. It was more likely that the critic was hoping to replace Kenneth Tynan at the Observer, but local press is so good for the ego!

The Rivals – Festival Players

FUN AND FLAMES

April 1950, back to Stamford for a wedding in St Michael's Church. Definitely with hat and gloves, even more definitely a frothy veiled concoction, my pink interview bowler consigned to the back of a cupboard.

Jo was marrying Gerald Clementson, a junior doctor at Tite Street. Their brief engagement led to my worst ever *faux pas.*

'Why the rush? You know what everyone will say.'

Jo blushed and smiled oddly.

'Shotgun weddings' were not for sensible people like us, suspicions were more likely to be voiced as gossip and sniggers behind hands. Six months later Geraldine arrived. How tactless can anyone be? A friend indeed!

Jo's wedding reception: Hazel Smith, Me,
Hazel Spencer, Brenda Hallas

Later in the year Beth and I made the first of several annual pilgrimages to Stratford-on-Avon for a week of theatregoing, sometimes queuing all night to see plays we hadn't managed to book in advance. We saw John Gielgud and Peggy Ashcroft in 'Much Ado About Nothing,' Gielgud and Barbara Jefford in 'Measure for Measure' and 'Julius Caesar.'

Other young actors whose names would become familiar - Robert Hardy, Alan Badel, Maxine Audley, Robert Shaw would often drink in the Dirty Duck, the actors' pub, its real name The Black Swan though no-one would recognise that name. It was always full of theatre lovers and others who simply hoped to mingle, however unnoticed, with the famous.

We had no tickets for Julius Caesar, so we planned to queue all night on Friday for the Saturday matinee before rushing to catch our train home. Impossible to leave without seeing Gielgud's Cassius. At lunchtime in the Dirty Duck, attempting to look nonchalant over our glasses of cider, we stared at the handsome young Welsh actor we'd already seen in Christopher Fry's 'Boy With A Cart.'
'Fancy a game of darts?'
The invitation came from a couple of students we'd met. Halfway through the contest I hit a never to be forgotten treble twenty and the bull, bang in the middle. There was a small burst of applause and I turned to give a mock curtsey to find myself facing John Gielgud, Peter Brook and the gorgeous Richard Burton. For the rest of the game I rarely threw a straight dart. Beth chalked up the meeting as the beginning of fame, but I doubt if they registered these two blushing young women for more than a few seconds,

After the evening performance of Henry VIII, we went to the stage door to meet a drama school friend of Beth's who was playing standard-bearers and similar major parts. A glass of cider at the Dirty Duck, then Michael Bates, later of Last of the Summer Wine fame, invited us all for drinks. His flat was upstairs, the room small and very warm, my glass strangely always full of pleasant-tasting water. Michael Bates sat next to me.
'My father works in the Colonial Office too.'
I wasn't being fooled by so obvious a chat-up line.
'And mine's the Prime Minister' I said.
Was there no end to my wit? I discovered on my return to work that his father *did* work there, at a much higher rank than mine. My stupidity may have cost me a love affair with the famous – but then again, perhaps not.

Around midnight we decided to leave to join the queue outside the theatre. I was fine until I stood at the top of Michael's stairs, which wobbled, looming and fading alarmingly. The 'water' had been gin, the glass regularly topped up and the gin was not happy with the cider I'd drunk earlier. Clinging to Beth, a far more sophisticated drinker who'd stuck to beer, I weaved my way to the theatre queue but spent the rest of the night polluting the Avon or in the Ladies, an amused Beth

escorting me once I could safely stand up. She stayed in the queue until the box office opened but I staggered back to the hotel.
'Try to eat something, it'll help.'
Whoops, watery scrambled egg, probably dried; no help at all. I fell into bed, waking at noon with an almighty hangover. Beth brought Alka Seltzer, then took me to the Dirty Duck, where the landlord recommended angostura bitters. Did I deserve such punishment? Worse was to come as I slept through most of Julius Caesar. We discovered later that Richard Burton was in Stratford to audition for the following season, when were to drool over his Ferdinand in The Tempest, Prince Hal in Henry IV and then Henry V. I stayed sober that season.
I confessed to Mum but surprisingly she said only
'Had to happen sometime. Don't make a habit of it.'

At the Webber Douglas New Year Ball early in January 1951 I whirled in Dashing White Sergeants, Eightsome Reels and Auld Lang Syne and downed a few – not enough to repeat my Stratford effort – gin and tonics before three of us took a taxi to Beth's bedsit in the warren of Gloucester Road houses converted to flats and bedsits.
2 a.m, the coldest hour of the night, the only heating a small gas fire with guttering pink and blue flames which ate shillings (5p, about the size of a 10p piece). Before folding ourselves into blankets on the floor, we danced round the cramped room until Bridget yelled
'Look out, Beth, your skirt's ...'

Too late, the layered net skirt had caught fire, flames shooting up around her. First Aid lessons taught that flames must be smothered, but no-one explained how a torch shrieking and rushing round in a confined space could be made to stand still long enough to be 'smothered.' I grabbed Beth's fur coat, her parents' Christmas gift, shoved her violently onto the bed and threw it over her. She lay whimpering and we were scared to look, aware only of the smell of singeing which was Beth's almost waist-length hair, now a tangle of varying lengths. Apart from deep shock, her only injuries were blisters on the backs of her hands; the satin underskirt must have been non-inflammable.

Tentatively we opened the door of her bedsit. Silence. I pulled up the window sashes to get rid of smoke and smell, saw a couple of lights in windows around the buildings. Not a sound. First Aid rules ordered hot, sweet tea. Bridget, a fellow Webber D student, boiled the kettle, her hands shaking almost too much to pour. Beth lay on her bed, covered in a clean sheet.

There was a payphone in the hall. Beth had stopped trembling.

'Shall we wake the housekeeper, or ring your parents?'.

'What housekeeper? If you two hadn't been here I'd have been a charred mess. They don't take any notice of shouting in Earls Court. And not my parents. I've ruined my gorgeous coat. Father will be furious.'

I knew Mr and Mrs Ross well enough to be sure their daughter's welfare would matter more than a coat, however expensive, but waking them at 5a.m. would cause disproportionate anxiety. Beth dozed but Bridget and I were wakeful, only too aware of what could have happened.

At 7.30 I rang Gerald, now an almost fully qualified doctor. He was reassuring.

'You did well. Get her to Casualty or a chemist soon.'

Half an hour later I knocked at the housekeeper's flat. She came to the door with sleep-encrusted eyes, hair in curlers, dressing gown loosely tied.

'Bit early, love. Locked yourself out?'

'Did you not hear the noise last night?'

I must have sounded accusing.

'Thought it was drunks rowing. What's happened? Got a dead body?'

'No, but we could have had.'

Five minutes later she was uniformed, hair combed, efficient and concerned.

'Does she need an ambulance? Any furniture damaged?'

'No to both, apart from her new coat and a few blisters.'

Relief all round, though I suspect the furniture was her priority. Bridget found cream for the blisters, there were a few on my hands too. Beth refused to leave her room until her hair had been washed and the singed ends trimmed. We heard no more about the coat and she seemed to recover completely, but in future we all steered well clear of gas fires.

Later that year the Festival of Britain opened on the south bank of the Thames. Partly commemorating the centenary of the 1851 Great Exhibition at Crystal Palace, the country was this time demonstrating our recovery both physically and economically from the war, though many cities were still in ruins. I was already infatuated by London, but now we had even more excitement. The site was dominated by amazing buildings, the Skylon, the Dome of Discovery, the cinema, later to become the National Film Theatre, the Royal Festival Hall, its red 'flying buttress' seats and huge organ pipes different from any concert hall I, or most people, had ever seen.

Beth was in her final term, preparing to become a mostly-out-of-work actress, her ambition to star in the musicals which filled West End theatres. School and wars seemed centuries away, the boys who'd been our friends now completing their National Service. Facing a few more months of boredom and uniform before going to University, they made a habit of spending weekend leaves in London and we spent the summer escorting many of them round the Festival. The worst part was the queues, as the entire population of the British Isles seemed to have gathered on the South Bank. There was so much to see, each meriting a separate queue. The amazing colours and patterns put wartime dinginess to shame. After exhausting hours standing around, then being dazzled by the imaginative displays, we were soon restored by dining and dancing in Soho restaurants.

Tickets for concerts at the Festival Hall sold out even before it opened, but it would still be there after the Festival ended. I became so familiar with the South Bank I could almost have applied to be a tour guide. I was less keen on the Festival Pleasure Gardens in Battersea Park, though John Moffatt, on his visit, begged to go there. I think he was teasing, remembering the day he and I were stuck for ages at the top of the Big Wheel at Stamford Fair the term before we left school. I'd seen the Rotor on a newsreel, people spinning round stuck to a wall in mid-air. Nothing would persuade me to try it, fairgrounds were not on my 'To do' lists.

Mum seemed to find my full social life difficult.
'You've been out to eat every Saturday this month.'
Was she envious? Much food was still rationed and she and Dad rarely ate out. For her and many other still reasonably young women the war had meant missing out on so much. But it was our turn now, the generation who had grown up with air raid sirens.

THEY CALL IT COMING OF AGE

At the end of January 1952 I rang the restaurant at the Dorchester Hotel, where I'd always longed to eat – or dine. 'I'd like to reserve a table for eight on February 9th for a 21st birthday dinner.'

'Certainly Madam. Will 7.30 be convenient? Have you any special requirements. A cake, champagne?'

Me, at the Dorchester, drinking champagne. No, you quaffed champagne. Why not? I was paying for most of it. Dad wouldn't like it – a beer or five at the local was his idea of a night out, but he was coming and no argument.

'That bloody school put ideas into her head. Places like that won't want us.'

Mum occasionally played mediator.

'Let her have her treat. They'll be glad enough to take our money.'

Apart from drinking at his local pub Dad was scared of any leisure activity that took place beyond his front door. Mum was equally worried, mainly about picking up the right knife and fork, but she liked the idea of dressing up and was almost as pretentious as I was fast becoming. I ordered two bottles of champagne but no cake. There would be cake at home on Sunday, my actual birthday when I was having a party for friends, but the highlight was to be this dinner at the Dorchester, close family and friends only. Beth couldn't see why my parents were making a fuss, but then the Ross family ate in hotels as regularly as the Fairmans had fish and chips indoors. I still needed to impress her, but it was unnecessary, we'd been best friends when I'd lived in pristine squalor in Stanley Street with its scullery and outside toilet.

On Wednesday 6th something unusual caught my eye from the office window. We could see the Houses of Parliament and the Union Jack was at half-mast. Mr Heptinstall, one of my two bosses, looked in from his room next door.

'The king's died' he said, 'In his sleep. Only 56, poor chap. It's been on the cards for weeks.'

How were we supposed to react? Royal weddings were for celebrations, we'd had days off school for Princess Elizabeth's and again when her son was born. But Royal deaths? Seven of us crowded into the tea-making room, mainly male senior civil servants who rarely saw the inside of this grubby space. Tea arrived on their desks ready-poured by the female staff. They agreed dark ties would be appropriate for a few days, including Saturday.

'And you young ladies?'

Was that me? I was rarely called lady, normally 'Miss Fairman' by all but my closest colleagues.

'Dark skirts or dresses, I think. If you *must* wear lipstick, keep it pale.'

Civil servants, however senior, still worked on Saturday mornings, when casual dress was permitted, the only time women could wear 'slacks.' Many of the men wore brown corduroy trousers and bright pullovers, often in hand-knitted fair-isle.

Right now people were phoning home to give the news to their wives. Our house had no phone and Mum was working at United Dominions Trust and personal calls were discouraged unless in a dire emergency. Early editions of the Evening News announced officially that, after a long illness his Majesty King George VI died in his sleep at the Royal Estate at Sandringham. Royalist or not, it was a sobering moment. The public was invited to view the lying-in-state in St Stephen's Hall.

'I shan't go.' Mr Heptinstall was fervently anti-royalist. 'You can if you must but I can only give you half an hour, the rest will have to come off your lunch hour.'

The department couldn't be expected to give away valuable working time and we knew there would be long queues. I wasn't interested in seeing a coffin and my lunch hour was precious, I'd rather spend it at the Tate Gallery or at a concert in St Margaret's Westminster.

As I arrived home Mum shouted from the kitchen before I'd closed the front door.

'Have you heard? You'll have to cancel the dinner.'

'Suppose so. Dad'll be pleased.'

Hotels and theatres dimmed their lights. Next morning shop windows were draped in black, men wore black ties and many of the women were in dark clothing. Somehow it seemed far more serious than wartime tragedies, perhaps because it was happening to only one family, a family we knew well but only from photographs or newsreels, we could afford to affect mourning. I rang to cancel dinner, offering to rebook later but knowing I never would. I have since dined twice at the Dorchester, both formal business occasions. The service was impeccable, the food a major disappointment.

On the afternoon of the Royal funeral Hep agreed reluctantly that three of us, without him of course, could watch the cortege as it passed through Parliament Square and down Whitehall. The flag-

draped coffin (the Union Jack or the Royal Standard – I suspect the latter) and the black horses with their scarlet plumes were superb, but it was the rhythm of the drums in that crowded silence that gripped me most. More curious than distressed, I watched as if it were a piece of theatre, which it was and trundled back to Victoria Street unmoved.
'Tea-time.'
Hep had actually boiled a kettle, a great concession.

Saturday was a non-event. Hep thought it ridiculous to cancel a 21st celebration for a mere King's funeral, but who else would have been celebrating that night? From the tone of the restaurant manager, the chef would be feeding only a few residents. Sunday's party at home was still on, but a further crisis intervened and the jellies remained soggy in their waxed dishes. Dad was taken ill; we fed him whisky to help his stomach pains but eventually Mum called an ambulance. Somewhat dramatically he emptied his pockets, thrusting all his loose change into my hand.
'If I don't come back, girl, it's yours.'

Dad collapsed and so did my birthday party. And of course he came back. The hospital diagnosed 'Drunk at daughter's 21st' and he was sent home on foot. Drunk yes, but on medicinal whisky and with an undiagnosed ulcer which had been made far worse by the alcohol. He seemed to recover and his health faded into an unimportant distance, like our memory of the weeping young princess who had so suddenly become a Queen.

Part of the group who commuted with Mum, Lesley and me from Bexleyheath included Ian, a manager of some kind. In May Ian invited us to join his family at the Trooping the Colour on Horse Guards Parade, to watch the as yet uncrowned Queen Elizabeth on one of her first public occasions. I willingly took a day's leave but Mum and Lesley declined. The day was memorable mainly for the behaviour of Ian's five-year-old son. His constant whimpers, scratching of pimples on his face, pulling at his jumper were irritating to others as well as me, though I tried politely to conceal it. I overheard
'Why bring the kid if he's not well?'
No Ian on the Saturday train; on Monday he apologised.
'I'm afraid Peter has chickenpox, we didn't know and he so wanted to see the horses. I expect you had it when you were his age?'
But I hadn't and a couple of weeks later a pounding headache and red blotches on my chest heralded a very nasty bout. Adults apparently have more serious reactions to childish illnesses and itching was an

inappropriate description of the compulsion to claw my face and head. I had long hair which quickly became entangled and enmeshed, but my temperature was too high to bath or to shampoo my hair. I wept from both pain and humiliation whenever I caught sight in a mirror of my red scabby face and gorse-bush head. Lennie, still living next-door, caught chickenpox too, though not from me. His girlfriend Sheila lived opposite us and her younger brother brought the infection home from school in a year which saw the worst outbreak in our part of London since before the war.

I was reproached by Dr Barrett for going to the surgery to be signed off. Those wondrous days when, if you weren't well you walked in and waited to see your own doctor!
'But the spots have gone. I want to go back to work.'
Dr Barrett had known me since birth, give or take a few years of wartime gaps.
'Young Margaret, you should know better, you're still infectious. The spots may have gone but you have several scabs. Work can wait another week. Go home and read a few more books instead of helping to infect all my patients.'

Miss Darlow retired. Her replacement, John King, was an utterly different character, a civil servant who had risen through the ranks. Far less intellectual or committed to his work, Mr King's main interest was photography. With Margaret Fairlie, my colleague who worked next door in Hep's office, I regularly spent summer lunch-hours modelling in St James' Park, all very conventional and definitely fully dressed. Mr King's interests lay in camera angles and light and shade, not the female form. Office conversations, pretty one-sided, became very boring, very little about colonial affairs, more camera clubs and hints of naughtier photos and activities in other venues.
I'd been in Social Services Department for almost three years and thought it was time for a change, although I was warned that, like daring children asking for sweets, I should wait to be offered.
Otherwise I risked being sent to an area no-one wanted, but I was determined.
The transfer was to Telegraphs, Codes and Cyphers, a 'chalk and cheese' situation.
'I did warn you,' Margaret Fairlie said, 'You'll be so bored. Did they tell you it's shift work?'
That was a major reason for accepting, an excuse to escape from home occasionally, but I was unwilling to listen to her doubts.

In this new department I met with true bureaucracy and regretted in many ways my hasty departure from the stimulation of Victoria Street. No more letter-writing, programme-planning, political discussions with dedicated and knowledgeable people. I was now working in the main building in Great Smith Street, part of a team of six managing around thirty other staff, the decoders, in a vast room. We worked in shifts. Team leaders were provided with a small bedroom and bathroom at the top of the building for optional sleepovers, in case a crisis arose in Africa or elsewhere and we were called on to deal with urgent telegrams.

Assistant Principals the grade above mine, usually Oxbridge and male, were resident for a week at a time, which they found extremely boring. I was often invited to share a bottle of wine in their sitting room, the young bachelors occasionally making tentative advances, the married ones often with their wives there to share the evening. At least I was usually busy, rather than sitting around until my shift ended at 10 p.m. On the other hand, although I now often slept in central London there was little time to enjoy any night life, as morning shifts began at 8. Apart from twelve hours on Christmas Day the Department never closed and I more than once offered to take the Christmas evening shift, when a special supper was delivered. It was far less tedious than staying at home.

We supervised the work of the decoding staff, distributed and on occasion decoded (or encoded) Top Secret telegrams. Excitement might be added to a shift by a De-you, where we assisted the relevant Minister, often wearing trousers hastily dragged over pyjamas, to decipher this one himself. The Official Secrets Act certainly applied to us; I had knowledge before the Press of such major issues as Archbishop Makarios and Enosis in Cyprus, Ian Smith in Rhodesia, Mau Mau in Kenya. Not quite John le Carre, but they were important years, although I was ignorant of my part in history and the opportunities I was given to witness policy-making. I worked under - a very long way under, never meeting them, Colonial Secretaries like Oliver Lyttleton (Tory) and Jim Callaghan (Labour) and was privy to many imprecations from senior Principals when policies they were required to follow differed widely from their own political leanings. They saw no need to lower their voices when a mere Executive officer, a young female at that, walked into their offices with an urgent telegram. Why would I have any interest in or understanding of what they were discussing? These moments made the job more lively, but I had to admit that Margaret had been right, I was bored.

A PROPER WOMAN AT LAST?

A year earlier the King's death had scuppered my 21st birthday and I wasn't going to let the Coronation slip by unnoticed. My friends and I decided the best position to see the spectacle would be from the Mall. Bad weather was forecast but we were young and hardy. After a hearty supper six of us set off, carrying bags with vital supplies: make-up remover, fresh make-up, apples and toothpaste. Sweet-scented smiles were vital for glamorous young women, three of them budding actresses.

A grey and drizzling twilight, but we were prepared. We spread the apples with toothpaste before sleeping and again in the morning. The make-up needs no explaining. The men had heroically lugged a tarpaulin with them, to drape over us all when we finally attempted sleep. Rain seeped underneath and it was bedraggled groupies who surfaced puffy-eyed around 6 a.m. The Mall was already buzzing, the young soldiers in their bearskins (never dare call them busbies, they insisted) standing to attention in front of us. To make sure we kept our places some of us stood guard while we queued in ones and twos at the already unpleasant temporary public loos. A minor crisis.
'Can anyone lend me a comb? I've forgotten mine.'
Beth of the long blonde mane forget her comb? Unheard of. It was I, well-trained in tidiness and hygiene, who disobeyed the rule of a lifetime,
'*Never* use someone else's comb, think what you might catch.'
Go away, Mum. My head survived and no awful itches ensued.

We heard there was television at some of the pubs on the route and a few less hardy spirits in the crowds deserted. June it might be, but certainly not 'flaming,' it was still wet and chilly but we'd not fidgeted and stamped out cramp half the night to miss the real thing. Around 9.30 the soldiers took breaks, which meant first standing at ease, then being sent behind us to take off their bearskins and use their latrines, strictly 'Forces only,' though the rest of us were permitted to share the smell. We flirty girls were quick to persuade them to let us try on the bearskins. If more senior ranks hovered the headgear was quickly snatched back. I was glad to be rid of mine, it was very heavy and the guardsman owner wasn't that appealing.

Newspaper sellers pushed through the crowds:
'Read all about it - Hillary climbs Everest.'

How clever to manage that on Coronation day. Except that he hadn't, the summit had been reached a few days earlier but had been embargoed, editors recognising the sales value of such headlines as
'What a Gift for the Queen.'
Our legs ached, we were tired and hungry but a wan sun forced its way through the frowning clouds and the landaus and open carriages began to leave Buckingham Palace, pageantry indeed. The service from Westminster Abbey was relayed on loudspeakers and Handel's 'Vivat Regina' echoed around us and on radios around the country and possibly the world. We waited patiently, we had little choice in those crowds, until the carriages returned from the Abbey, naming those faces we recognised. Princess Margaret, with far more delicate features than the best photographer could capture, the huge Queen of Tonga, young Prince Charles and Princess Anne with their nanny gaining 'Oohs and Aahs' from the sycophantic crowds.
Bushes in St James's Park and a certain lack of modesty had to serve our basic needs until we were finally able to stagger free, walking as far as Tottenham Court Road to find a café with seats, hot drinks and a chance to wash our hands and other euphemisms in private.
Beth's energy was restored.
'Let's finish this off with a celebration party. Come on Mags, your place is perfect. We'll be good this time, promise. Brownies' honour.'
Beth was never a Brownie, but I loved parties and was now living in South Hill Park Gardens, near Belsize Park in Hampstead.

I'd escaped from Bexleyheath a few months earlier, when Jo and Gerald suggested I move into the empty bedsit on the floor below their flat in Belsize Park. Not an entirely altruistic invitation as I provided them with a handy babysitter, but I loved their two little ones and Mum could find no cause for objection. I had a large room with a single divan doubling as a seat during the day. There was a thick pale rug, too easily made grubby, where I sprawled with a book in front of the gas fire to keep warm on cold nights, assuming I'd saved enough shillings to feed the greedy meter. An anteroom, probably a dressing room when this large Victorian villa housed only one family, had been converted into a kitchen with gas and a sink but no water. This had to be carried in large jugs from the bathroom four stairs below, shared with another bedsit girl. Jo and Gerald's flat took up the whole top floor.

My first guests were my parents, who naturally arrived early, criticising the dust they'd not left me time to mop but reluctantly praising my cooking. I'm not of Wheelband stock for nothing, my Grandmother and her sister bequeathed me their cooking genes. The next time I entertained was on Beth's birthday, celebrated as only she and her actor friends could, with far too much to drink and queues for the bathroom, not always reached in time. We cleaned up next day but the landlady, who lived in the basement, decreed no more alcohol at parties and a midnight curfew. Her only previous rule had been

'You can bring a man home as long as you don't make a noise and he isn't black.'

I don't remember arguing, it possibly hardly registered even though I was working in the Colonial office and meeting West Indians, though not socially, every day. Advertisements for 'Rooms to Let' frequently and quite legally stated

'No blacks, no Irish, no children.'

After the May debacle I was unsure how my landlady would feel about allowing another party so soon, but as an extreme Royalist she could hardly refuse this tribute to the great day. I promised no drunken antics, warning Beth not to invite her more outrageous friends. This left us short of men, but not for long. I'd been observing, discreetly from behind my curtains the young men who lived in the ground floor flat opposite. I heard broad Australian accents and counted around five regulars, but noticed few women. I knew they owned an ancient car.

A car. Now there was a find, I could do with a car in my life. Jo came with me to ring the bell. Her wedding ring, milk-stained jumper, pram dragged daily up and down the steps, were unmistakable traces of motherhood and offered an air of respectability, proof that we weren't running a house of ill-repute.

The door was opened by a tall, dark, handsome prince, well-spoken despite the accent. Too nervous to listen to what he said, I gabbled my script.

'I... We... live opposite,' then it came out in a nervous rush 'We-wondered-if-you'd-all-like-to-come-to-a-party-on-Saturday.' Take a breath, slow down. 'To celebrate the Coronation.'

Politeness forced me to add 'Girlfriends too.'

'Good evening.'

He extended a hand. Quaint Colonial manners.

'I'm John. Come and meet the others. Would you like a cup of tea?'
Jo excused herself, she'd done her bit, I seemed to have passed
the test.
'No thanks, children to feed, my husband's on duty in an hour.'
She made Gerald sound more like a policeman than a junior doctor.
John led me into the sitting room.
'This is... sorry, I didn't catch your name.'
Like some tongue-tied adolescent I attempted wit.
'I didn't throw it.'
No-one laughed, but nor was I summarily evicted.
'I'm having a party and we're short of – I mean would you like to
come – it's good to welcome tourists from the empire – I've always
wanted to meet Australians.'
They weren't openly offended.

Handshakes and grins all round, then
'I'm from New Zealand. Unfortunately I have an engagement this
weekend, so please excuse me.'
John's tone was cool. Later one of the others explained that Kiwis
found it essential to clarify the difference, so that we Poms
understood New Zealanders were the cream of the Antipodes. His
manners and vocabulary were certainly old Colonial. Class warfare
from down under?
I remember their names, their home towns and accents, as regional
as in Britain. Bruce number one, stocky and phlegmatic, his accent
the mildest, was from Melbourne. The quiet one, another Bruce,
was from pre-Opera house but already fashionable Sydney. A
second John, Aussie John this time, surname Stewart, known to all
as 'Stew.' Long, lanky and cynical he'd travelled from Brisbane,
home of both the opal and the least attractive accent.

Finally Stew's pal, also from Brisbane, a Steve McQueen look-alike.
'Howard Longland. You have a name, I take it?'
He could take anything he wanted. I had never, ever felt like this,
arms tingling, legs shaky. So that's why falling in love was
sometimes called chemistry, a physical reaction when two elements
make contact.
'I'm Margaret – well, Maggie.'
My throat constricted, he was still holding my hand.
'We'd love to come, we'll bring bottles. What time?'
'Eight-ish. And we can't make a noise after midnight.'
I sounded like a kid with strict parents, but now wasn't the time to
explain the row after Beth's birthday 'Do.'

The party was probably successful, nibbles, wine, beer and cigarette smoke and no-one was sick. For me there was only Howard. We talked non-stop, not touching, we didn't need to yet, possibly didn't dare. As midnight chimed Stew rounded them up.
'Time to go, men. Got the glass slipper, Howard?'
So it had been that obvious.

Howard Longland

They thanked me, adding an invitation to join them in a trip to the Broads the following weekend. Howard frowned as I accepted
'I'm working next weekend.'
Would it look too obvious if I turned them down? Probably. Besides, I liked them all and I'd never seen the Norfolk Broads.

Mum was duly horrified.
'You don't know them. They're foreigners, they might molest you.'
Delicious word, I'm sure 'rape' would never have forced its way past her dentures. For women of my mother's generation and background despite, or maybe because of, living through two world wars, anyone who crossed the sea or even the Scottish or Welsh borders to live in England was 'not like us' and therefore probably up to no good. I ignored her well-meant warnings, I was not going to miss this weekend and on Saturday climbed into their ancient car. In some ways I was relieved that Howard was absent. His proximity would be unbearable, as I knew already from the evenings that week when he'd come for a meal. They'd been reasonably chaste (it *was* 1953), but only just.

The men were charming companions and I mourned Howard's absence less than I'd expected. We stopped in Long Melford for lunch, explored the surrounding Suffolk villages and found a B&B in Lavenham. Next morning as we neared the Broads the car began to cough. When steam belched from below the bonnet Stew decided to stop and get help.

'Big end,' announced the AA man gloomily, 'Couple of days at least.'

He arranged a tow to the nearest garage but from then on we were stranded, three men and a girl far from a station, a town or even a pub. A guardian angel, a farmer driving a jeep, turned up, offered us lunch with his family and a lift to the nearest main road to hitchhike back to London. The car could be picked up the following weekend.

The farm was vast, the main crop opium grown, with a Government licence, for medicinal purposes. We sat in sun loungers drinking very large tumblers of gin before a pre-lunch tour of the acres. Little of the tour was memorable, apart from one sentence.

'Please don't say the fields remind you of Flanders,' our host begged, 'I swore I'd floor the next one.'

He was safe. I wasn't old enough to remember Flanders and I doubted if the Aussies had heard of it, Gallipoli was their Flanders. His wife filled our rucksacks with bags of home-made cakes before we left for the next stage of this adventure.

I began to pine for Howard. Like all love-struck damsels I wanted to talk about him all the time, yet something told me this was unwise. The others seemed to have embargoed his name. Did he have another woman, or even women, somewhere? Did they disapprove of me? Had the group foresworn complications which might affect their world tour? Howard had warned me they were leaving for Canada before Christmas, but it was still early summer and I refused to think beyond the next few days.

Our generous host set us down at a spot he assured us was good for lifts and the three men pulled straws to see who was to be my partner. Flattering? Not really, they explained that a man and a woman together were more likely than two men to be offered a lift. Obvious, if I'd used my head instead of my vanity. Bruce from Sydney stayed behind with Stew while Melbourne Bruce and I walked a few hundred yards along the verge. Five minutes later the others waved and grinned at us from a lorry, but we hadn't long to wait before a car pulled up and a friendly couple gave us a long ride, taking us almost into London.

From there it was public transport and to our mutual amazement as we stepped out of the tube at Belsize Park, further down the platform Bruce and Stew were leaving the same train, an almost unheard of ending to a hitchhiking journey. Having had several short hops from drivers attracted by the Australian emblems on their backpacks, the other two were certain we were miles behind. I suspect they were disappointed; England had won the Ashes, we weren't allowed to be experts at hitchhiking too.

Howard opened the door.

'Kettle's on, come in.'

His questions about the trip and the car were directed mainly at his friends but his eyes were almost permanently on me.

Next evening he came to my flat and invited me to a film, I've no idea what film and a couple of weeks later he proposed.

I visited my former colleagues in Victoria Street to share my news, Mr Heptinstall commenting cynically but presciently that he'd believe it when I had a ring.

'You'll find young men on post-war travels make piecrust promises in triplicate.'

Howard caused my first major heartbreak. I made the mistake of sleeping with him. I'd left Hampstead and gone back to Bexleyheath, partly to help out with debts my parents had acquired, but possibly also to protect my innocence. Spending Saturday night with a passionate boyfriend in his flat when all the other residents were away was not highly sensible and I succumbed.

Howard's family in Brisbane was well-known and wealthy. When he was ten his mother had left his father, then three years later her next husband, in notorious tabloid scandals. Traumatised and still angry, he seemed torn between rampant attempts to, as he put it 'corrupt' me and determination to marry a virgin. His reaction to our night of passion shocked me. In less than a week he seemed disappointed and almost disgusted with me, as if I were some kind of scarlet woman. He needed someone who could stay on a pedestal despite him. I hadn't even enjoyed it that much, it had been quite painful, but I was still very much in love.

A month or so later at a party I disturbed him in a back room, kissing an Australian ex-girlfriend. My stomach clenched, I felt sick, returned to the main party but couldn't bear to speak to anyone. I went to get my coat, passing Howard on the way to the door.

'Hey, leaving early? Why?'

He laughed when I told him.

'Don't be stupid, she's an old friend.'

But he didn't stop me. I kept away from Hampstead, sobbed myself to sleep, snapped at my mother. Then, horror of horrors, I began feeling sick. Mum would hover outside the bathroom in the mornings but it was either a false alarm or a very early miscarriage.

Howard wrote asking to meet before he left for Canada. He was shocked that I'd suspected pregnancy and considered abortion, neither legal nor cheap. Conversation was stilted, he asked

'How could you destroy my child?'

'Easily, under the circumstances.'

He assured me again that the kiss had been only friendly. I didn't quite believe him, he'd allowed me to leave and made no attempt to redeem our relationship, but his concern about a baby made me feel a little better about him. He wrote twice from Canada, not exactly love letters and I began to hope I was recovering.

In April I flew to Paris, my first venture abroad, with a friend from Bexleyheath, Anita. We were proper tourists, except that we avoided the Eiffel Tower, preferring the Left Bank with its hordes of artists. We bought very smelly cheeses, so strong we had to put them on the window ledge outside our room. Our favourite haunts were Montmartre and the Sacré Coeur, where we met two French students who brightened our days, though both my student and Anita were annoyed that I could rouse no enthusiasm for physical shenanigans. Anita disappeared in a huff for a night, I didn't need to ask where. Next day she asked

'Isn't the point of Paris romance with a Frenchman?'

'Sorry. I didn't realise. You should have warned me.'

Howard and I met once more on his way back to Australia. The spark was still there, but fading. I'd told him about Paris in one of my letters.

'Sorry I cramped that Frenchie's style'

he said ruefully.

We kissed goodbye and I never got to experience the poisonous Queensland spiders. In several ways I'd had a very lucky escape

A few weeks later I developed a painful rash, spent a couple of days in bed and Mum sent for Dr Barrett.

'Morning my dear. Haven't seen you since chickenpox. More scabs? Let's have a look.'

86

He peered briefly at my torso. Completely clear, but my arms and legs looked repulsive and itched almost as much as the chickenpox. He tapped Howard's photo on my bedside table.

'Handsome young man. Important, then?'

'I don't want to talk about it.'

'Looks to me like a broken heart.'

I could only nod. Howard had left London – and me. Mr Heptinstall had been right, a real engagement would have meant a ring on my finger.

Dr B explained the probable link between the rash and the heartbreak. Before his time?

'The rash should go in about six weeks, you'll be ready for a new and more reliable young man by then.'

He was right about the rash but I've unfortunately never really been interested in reliable men.

ENTER THE HERO

A Monday in October 1955. The last to arrive at rehearsal with The Festival Players, I was in no mood for 'Much Ado About Nothing.' Like my life, except that *that* was little ado, definitely about nothing, a tedious crawl between office and home. Evenings in dull pubs with equally dull men, rehearsals, theatre and occasional parties marginally more exciting. Peter, the current dull man had announced the previous evening that our relationship had a serious future. It was typical of men (all two of them before Peter) to assume without asking that their undying love was reciprocated.

Peter and I met at a party where I knew few other guests and was sitting alone. A deep well-modulated voice asked
'May I join you? I'm Peter.'
Tall, young face, bald head crisscrossed with deep scars, he extended his hand. A new approach; my usual escorts didn't bother with formal handshakes. I never found out how he got the scars, only that he'd spent his National Service as a pilot and
'That was where my head got burnt.'
His mother was a psychiatrist, Peter in analysis
'Recovering from her parenting.'

Peter aimed (his words) to improve my cultural awareness, ignoring my own extensive knowledge of theatre and film, though he did introduce me to live opera which I'd been longing to see since I'd been enthralled by it in the fever hospital. Our visit to 'The Magic Flute' at Convent Garden was spoilt by Peter's odd meanness. Extremely expensive tickets, but time spent searching for a free parking place (pre-meter days, but private car parks in central London charged) almost made us late. Peter decided I didn't need a programme, so I watched three large women and an equally large man prancing around the stage. Not exactly broadening my culture as I hadn't the faintest idea what was going on, but the music was indeed magical and I fell in love with Papageno, sung by the superb Geraint Evans.

Peter was not only a deeply committed Catholic, but also a pretty fragile individual. We developed a habit of Sunday lunch at Peter's flat, then striding through Richmond Park arguing about Catholicism. A couple of weeks earlier he'd wept on my shoulder after we'd seen Frank Sinatra in 'The Man with the Golden Arm,' declaring that until he met me he was planning to become a monk. I panicked; I had no wish to be a barrier to his spiritual path. Moving rapidly from the confession to planning our future, he reckoned I needn't become a Catholic.

'You'd only need to agree to bring up the children in the faith.'

'If it's not right for me, why would I foist this mumbo-jumbo onto my children? You know nothing about me.'

I was furious and had no intention of marrying him, especially after the monk episode and was looking for both an excuse and the courage to dump him.

Among the regulars at that night's rehearsal were a couple of new faces, one new face in particular. A lock of dark curls covered his forehead, highlighting large grey eyes and cheekbones redefining the word hollow. He wore a spotted bow tie, chunky grey sweater, black needle-cord trousers. Pretentious, I thought. With those looks, those clothes, he had to be a brilliant actor planning to turn professional once his talent was recognised. The women were swarming round him and I immediately decided he wasn't my type. Not that Peter was my type either, and I knew I had to tackle the guilt of telling him. Guilt, my constant companion; I was a convert-in-waiting for the feminism about to burst on the western world. Eileen Butler our Director, a former Old Vic actor introduced the newcomers.

'Meet Gerry and Stan. Let's hear you two read. They may be only small parts, but they are still important. Stan, you go first.'

Stan, a fairly nondescript bank clerk, was competent enough. I was mildly surprised when Gerry stood up, I'd expected six feet of muscle, but he wasn't much taller than me. It wasn't his fault he looked like James Dean, though I suspected he was careful to emphasise the similarity. I was pouring myself a coffee when I heard Eileen's

'A little louder darling, no need to be nervous.'

'Darling' was mumbling, his legs twisting like a small boy wanting to pee and not knowing how to ask. We held our breaths. Eileen said brusquely she'd use him as a messenger or something. How had I got it so wrong, how could he look so right and yet be so hopeless?

As I collected my coat I joined the crowd craning over Gerry. Now what was he doing? Then I saw. A brilliant sketch of Beatrice and Benedict. Right costume, wrong role, not an actor but an artist. I was impressed and said so. He shrugged.

'It's the only thing I do. I'm only here because Stan dragged me.'

I wasn't immediately converted to Gerry-worship. My relations with Peter more strained than ever, I would join the group for a drink after rehearsals but was hardly its most lively member. Gerry appeared not to notice my reticence but often sat next to me in the pub, quietly offering his opinions of the films and plays he saw. So he was not only a talented artist, but a culture-vulture too! I decided he was either very shy or totally uninterested in me sexually. I was more used to men's attempts to charm me with unsubtle flattery, referring to my 'beautiful smile,' as in
'You have a beautiful smile, I'd like to see more of it,' their eyes focused slightly lower on my anatomy.

A few weeks later Eileen asked me to check that everyone was free for an extra Friday rehearsal. When I asked Gerry he pouted, very prettily though,
'It's the Eltham Drama Club annual dance.'
Did he imagine this would excuse him? He didn't know Eileen. I teased him.
'You wouldn't let us down at this late stage?'
'I was going to invite you to the dance with me.'
I was both amused and flattered; the 'artist' label and the grey eyes ensured that any unattached (and one or two attached) women in the group would have jumped at the chance. Why me? I'd not consciously encouraged him, officially I was 'attached' and I'd earmarked Gerry for a friend who was currently footloose. Intrigued, I persuaded Eileen to cancel the rehearsal.

I surprised myself by the hours I window-shopped for a dress, finally choosing an electric blue taffeta dream, neckline not too plunging, low-waisted, full-skirted, its swirling hem boosted by three net underskirts. Then I spent two agonising days walking around in new black patent stilettos, not so high I would tower over Gerry. On the day of the dance I rushed home to change, more teenager than sophisticated twenty-something. Why was I so nervous?
Gerry danced well, his quiet voice a change from my squabbles with Peter. He confessed
'I'm dreading "Much Ado," I've considered developing flu.'.
'You're joking, you've only got about five lines.'
'Don't worry, I'll be there. Can't have you angry with me.'
He knew how to charm a woman. After the last waltz he walked me to my train, kissed me chastely on the cheek. He rang me at work

on Saturday morning.

'No reason, just want to hear your voice. Fancy a Sunday stroll?'
Sundays meant lunch with Peter. Gerry sounded disappointed, then
'If Peter is so important why spend the last hour talking to me?'
Ouch! He went on
'Come and see "Waiting for Godot" on Tuesday.'

Everyone wanted tickets for this amazing new play. Peter and I had
already seen it, but that didn't stop my agreeing immediately. I
would have gone to any old rubbish Gerry suggested. This time
Godot was a very different experience. Peter followed Harold
Hobson's recommendations in The Sunday Times, but he'd
disagreed with Hobson's view, describing both Samuel Beckett and
the play as
'Pretentious Irish drivel.'
After the theatre Gerry and I strolled hand-in-hand along the
Thames Embankment talking non-stop, dissecting the play, all
Beckett's work, art, politics, cinema, music, each other, skating over
past or current loves. As we stood looking across at the Festival
Hall he sang *almost* as well as his idol Frank Sinatra 'London by
Night is a Wonderful Sight.'
We caught the last train with seconds to spare, he walked me
home, kissed me lightly on the lips, then stared at me
'Can I paint you one day?'
Kissing me again he left. It would take him an hour to walk home. I
was hooked.

This relationship was serious from the first, yet I'd never been so
confused. We were totally comfortable together, but he'd made
none of the sexual moves I was used to fending off. Old-fashioned
courtship? Or was he teasing, wanting me to be desperate for him?
I was happy to wait to find out, but before I went to bed I wrote to
Peter, explaining that I'd met someone else. Hasty? Cowardly? I
thought a rival would be more acceptable than being cast off for
being boring, too controlling and a Catholic. Three days later a thick
envelope arrived, containing the casual notes, the birthday and
Christmas card I'd sent him and an angry letter accusing me of
breaking his heart. A few months later his engagement was
announced in The Times. Short-lived heartbreak, then.

Gerry went home to Birmingham for Easter but came back to take
me to the Easter Parade in Hyde Park. Among the gaudy Easter
bonnets he announced

'I told Mother about you, said I wanted to marry you.'
Terrified, I laughed it off; it was too soon but I didn't immediately push him away. At Whitsun I went to meet his family. I had mixed feelings about meeting his mother, who sounded a pretty powerful lady. She was, but I loved her from the minute she first hugged, then embarrassed me.
'Call me Marjorie. You're staying with my friend Vinnie. My spare bedroom is far too untidy.'
Vinnie Guck added a fantastic word to our vocabulary, 'Gucky,' loud and tasteless. Within ten minutes of meeting her I'd had a demonstration of a cocktail cabinet with interior lighting and miniatures of every imaginable drink, been invited to admire the curtains, the furniture, told how much they'd cost; all hideous. Vinnie was kind, hospitable, generous, but I'm afraid we laughed at her behind her back, careful to keep it behind Marjorie's back too or we'd have been berated, quite rightly, for our appalling rudeness. Later in summer we made the first of several visits to Glyndebourne to see 'The Marriage of Figaro,' meeting his parents there.

Glyndebourne 1956

Marjorie apparently told Gerry he should grab me while he could as 'You'll never find another like her.'
Prophetic words? Certainly in reverse, there were surely few men like Gerry. Or perhaps not, judging from tales I heard much later from other divorced women.

LIKE A HORSE AND CARRIAGE?

Mum had said only a few months earlier,
'You're too choosy, you'll never get married if you don't look sharp.'

Comments like this came whenever I admitted that a boyfriend, however casual, had been sent on his way. Marriage was the only approved ambition for a girl in the Fifties, the theme of Pride and Prejudice definitely still ruled. When I announced that Gerry and I were engaged I thought I might have got it right for once. Mum's eyes sparkled, I expected an

'At last!'

but what she said was

'Will you find him too quiet for you?'

'He's just shy, he isn't quiet with me.'

'When's the happy day?'

'We thought October, it's a good time for tax breaks.'

Dad laughed, he loved a practical man and assumed it must have been Gerry's idea. As it happened, it was, I was more romantic about weddings, but also impatient. Marriage would be a legitimate, guilt-free reason both to leave home and to have sex.

'There'll be a lot to do. I suppose you're all right to have a white wedding?'

Was Mum being unusually tactful or simply prurient? October was five months ahead so it was unlikely to be a shotgun wedding, but she couldn't resist checking.

The whole engagement and wedding seemed to belong to everyone but us. Marjorie came to London with samples of rings. She worked for a jeweller in Birmingham, which meant she would get a discount. Holding Gerry's hand in the back seat of a prospective mother-in-law's car, examining rings as she passed them over her shoulder was not the romantic event I'd imagined. No connoisseur of diamond rings, I finally settled on a solitaire. Marjorie was delighted, saying

'Thought you'd choose that one, it's the most expensive.'

Mortified, I went to grab another, but she explained how it showed my good taste

'I've told that son of mine to treat you properly. He can afford it, not like when Gordon and I got married.'

She insisted too that I had a 22 carat gold wedding ring,

'Much better quality, my dear.'

Quality or not, it was a mistake, I had the ring engraved with our initials and the wedding date, but the markings wore off within a few years. Gerry's brother Tony was more sensible, or his fiancée Elizabeth was braver and they bought their rings privately. Marjorie failed to understand, though I did. Liz still has clear engravings on her 9 carat ring!

We celebrated the official engagement day, plus ring, with Gerry's family in Birmingham. They left us alone in the front room with a tray of tea in the best china cups and a vase of tiny red roses. Marjorie was so affectionate I couldn't object, wasn't sure I wanted to. It was rare to be in a loving family, but it was perhaps an early warning sign. Her wishes always came first and faced with dominant women I always buttoned my lips. I wonder where I learned that?
Every spare minute that summer was spent either in wedding preparations or in finding somewhere to live.

In 1956 few couples from our social backgrounds took out a mortgage as soon as they married. Our parents owned their homes, but not until they'd spent years in rented accommodation and had reliable incomes. Nostalgic for my Hampstead bedsit, I'd have preferred to spend a year or so in a flat nearer central London, but five years of cramped bedsits, with irate or pleading landladies regularly warning him to clean the place, had left Gerry wanting his own home and privacy. It matched his proud announcement to Dad that in the last tax year, 1954-5 he'd earned his first £1000, a sum Dad had never matched. My annual salary, in the fairly prestigious Executive Grade of the Civil Service, was £620, so £1000 was impressive.

We had no idea how to go about buying a house, but Gerry had colleagues who pointed us in the direction of estate agents. The newest trend was architect Eric Lyons' Span estate in Blackheath, houses with first floor sitting rooms and, even newer, flats for sale. Gerry's friend John Edwards, a surveyor, warned us that buying a leasehold flat was a fairly new idea and might not pay off in terms of insurance or property values. Ignorant in this field, we accepted John's expertise, though I would have loved to begin my married life in fashionable Blackheath.

We eventually chose a not-yet built house in Castlewood Drive, Eltham, with a garage and part-central heating but on an unimpressive estate not dissimilar to Gipsy Road. One of a row of six, the flat rooves of the garages formed the front gardens, as the houses were built into the side of a hill and backed onto woodland. Floors were to be covered in lino tiles to the buyer's specification. Luxury indeed. The builders must have cursed such freedom being offered to an artist, no plain grey or cream for us. The kitchen floor was mainly black, with yellow and white tiles inset in an interesting design, to match the Denby kitchenware we'd requested for wedding presents. In the 'through-room,' a post-war innovation with sitting and dining areas in one long room, Gerry designed an even more intricate pattern in black, red and white tiles and the hall was a mosaic of primary colours. When we moved in we papered the staircase and hall with wallpaper resembling newsprint, though rather more expensive.

As we were saving for a honeymoon there was no summer holiday. 'Much Ado' had been performed before Easter and, far too busy to learn new lines, I opted out of the next production. Wedding dresses, wedding breakfasts (an odd name as they usually took place in the afternoon,) arguments over guest lists provided more in the way of stage management and drama than any Shakespeare. In addition we had our daily jobs, form-filling for estate agents, visiting the half-built house, planning a honeymoon.
Tired and confused, I wondered more and more whose wedding it was, what on earth I was doing marrying at all, but I assumed all brides had their doubts. There was no point in asking our parents' advice, neither couple seemed a role model for happy marriages but all four would probably have dismissed any qualms. Marriage and family were surely the height of a girl's ambition, looking after a man the price she paid for security (and sex, if she was a 'nice' girl.)

We were coming up to the starting gate; the wedding was to be at St Michael's, Welling, our parish church, though none of my family had ever attended a service there. Couples were asked to attend three pre-nuptial lectures. At the first the Vicar's frown confirmed his disapproval of this secular couple. He suggested sourly that we might attend at least one service to hear the Banns read. We promised. Gerry muttered into my ear
'Told you we should have gone to a Registry Office.'

Beth and I had a girls' night out where I confessed my anxieties. 'It's only a year since I first set eyes on him and in a few weeks we'll be stuck together for ever. I was so sure, but now I'm more scared than excited.'

A brief lecture followed, hard-hitting but wise.

'You've always run away from men, even when we were still at school. I used to think you were fickle, but it's not that. You're scared of being loved. Howard wasn't the end of the world, we've all had broken hearts, sweetie. If you don't let yourself love this one there may not be another chance. I've seen the two of you together. It's just stage-fright. It'll be all right on the night. You always tell me that when I'm in pieces after dress rehearsals. Now – another gin and tonic and stop wittering.'

Beth always made me feel better.

October 20 1956:
Gordon, Marjorie, Janet, Tony, Gerry, Me, Beth, Mum, Dad,

MARRIAGE AND ALL THAT JAZZ

e kept the honeymoon venue secret, one of the few times I knew Gerry to defy his mother, who hated not knowing our destination. He'd spent time as a student painting in Tintagel and longed to go back. I was more than happy to agree, the sea and the Arthurian setting sounding highly romantic.

Stag nights, usually in the local pub, were traditionally held on the wedding eve. To avoid any danger of losing the rings, Dad offered to hang on to them and deliver them to Gerry's flat next morning before they left for the church. He came back grinning.

'You were right, Mick – Gerry can't take his booze, he's got an almighty hangover. Hope he remembers where the church is.'

Gerry was no drinker but his friends had plied him with a mixture of beer and spirits, to give him

'A great send-off.'

Huh.

As we left for the church I asked Dad if I looked pretty. Stupid of me.

'Pretty ugly.'

Did he really think that was funny? Couldn't he just for once have genuinely been affectionate and praised me? Yet I know, because one of our neighbours told me, that he boasted about me and my 'braininess', exaggerating my position at work. This must partly explain why I became a workaholic, the frantic need to succeed and the speed with which I sense failure.

As Dad walked me up the aisle to Bach's Toccata and Fugue in D I did feel special and a little awed, but it didn't last. During the ceremony I knelt on my dress, trapping it. Gerry and the Vicar had to help me to my feet, leading to stifled giggles even from the Vicar, which broke any tension. In the car taking us to the reception Gerry confided

'I feel sick. Could I get away without the speech?'

I felt a mixture of sympathy and irritation, but it wasn't his fault. His speech was charming, if subdued. We were feeling more relaxed as we changed into our 'going-away' clothes, the first time we'd been alone together in a hotel bedroom. Gerry, still pale, managed a grin.

 'And there's not even time to celebrate, but it's pretty tempting.'

So the hangover hadn't completely put him off me!

Not that I had any doubts, even though we'd agreed to be old-fashioned and wait until we were married to begin our wild sex life. My experience with Howard left me more than happy to agree.

Fashion 1956 – Going-away outfits plus cake!

Tony drove us to Falconwood Station in Marjorie's car, now festooned with tin cans and bunting. Their jangling embarrassed him, may have influenced his own very quiet but intimate and charming wedding to Liz a few months later. I wondered if everyone on the platform had heard us arrive. Would they guess why we were carrying new suitcases labelled 'Tintagel, Cornwall?' Surely not.

There was time for strong black coffee as we waited at Waterloo for our train to Salisbury. No-one could expect trains to run to Cornwall on a Saturday in October, so we were staying for two nights in Salisbury. Not wishing to be identified at the hotel as newly-weds, our very shiny rings, new clothes and suitcases and my hesitation in signing 'Smith' on the Register naturally offering no clue, I carefully swept the spare confetti into the wastepaper bin. I naively failed to consider that the maid would empty it next day, but then I was unused to hotel bedrooms. At breakfast I imagined sniggers behind the hands of every member of staff and was relieved to leave for the station on Monday.

Gerry had chosen well, Tintagel was then an ancient one-street Cornish village with a ruined castle and a long history to explore. As the sole out-of-season guests it was very obvious we were honeymooners. We were given the best bedroom, with huge windows overlooking wild Cornish waves. Small seaside villages offered few evening attractions out of season (and not too many in season) apart from the local pub and Gerry had had his fill of pubs. We spent hours playing table-tennis in the 'Games Room,' our hosts as smirking spectators, sharing with us evening cocoa and biscuits at ten, when we finally, without too much shyness could retire to bed. Their grins and 'sleep well' wishes did not help.

There was no morning lingering with a 'Do Not Disturb' notice on the door. We went out soon after breakfast every day, our main companion the hotel's giant German shepherd, self-appointed guard dog to guests as well as the building. The wizard Merlin himself might have envied his secret ways of lying in wait for us. Dogs are supposed to add to the pleasure of cliff-top walking, but not when their hobby is chasing sheep or diving suddenly between the legs of the innocent visitor gazing out to sea from the cliff edge. I was more than once threatened with early widowhood and I suspect that, had a farmer with a shotgun noticed our futile attempts to protect the sheep, the dog might never have returned home. We'd wanted a quiet week and apart from these minor irritations we absorbed the peace of the place, although Cornish autumn wind and rain offered more Jamaica Inn than sunlit Riviera.

We returned home anticipating the move into our brand new house, except that it was incomplete, still needing many fittings. A highly uncomfortable week followed, with my parents ceremoniously giving us their bedroom, the only one with a double bed, although they stopped short of tying ribbons across the doorway. Gerry returned to work, I had a few more days' leave which I spent at the Eltham house begging the builders to hurry. Staying at Gipsy Road was excruciating, Mum would cook dinner and sit watching us while we ate. We slept chastely; in that small house every sound carried and a smirking Dad brought us tea every morning, the only time I remember his doing that for anyone.

I finally issued an ultimatum. Whether or not it was ready, we were moving to Castlewood Drive. The radiators and hall flooring could be installed around us. The builders reluctantly agreed and we were IN, plus clothes, favourite childhood treasures, mountains of books, records and wedding gifts. These included a king-size bed, our two armchairs and enough towels to last our marriage.

The surfeit of towels was the result of a frantic call from Marjorie a few weeks before the wedding.

'My friends are asking what is left on your list that they would be happy buying. They don't understand some of these fancy things you've asked for.'

I was a little irritated. Our tastes were fashionable, not fancy.

'Try towels, we don't seem to have many. Colours are on the list.'

Now we had twenty, almost too many to fit into the airing cupboard. All sizes, soft and fluffy in the shades we'd wanted, the white ones stored for the future nursery use I took for granted. Our wedding gift list had included among various accessories a coat rack with coloured knobs which matched the hall tiles. The vivid colours, introduced during the Festival of Britain, were a farewell to khaki and blackouts, in the same way that Dior's New Look had compensated us for the wartime shortage of dress material.

Mum and Dad were our first guests. They came for Sunday lunch and a beady-eyed inspection, telling us unnecessarily how much hard work would be needed. The cheques we'd been given had provided a dining table, but we had to make do with two old chairs Gerry's mum gave us, a five-gallon oil drum covered in a blanket and a packing case ditto. I'm sure the Aunt who gave us the blankets hadn't expected them to end up as temporary dining chair covers. Books were ranged round the skirting boards on planks supported by bricks, bookshelves ordered but not yet delivered. They would be imported from Sweden, ultra-modern with black slatted sides.

'You'll have to knuckle down to housework, houses don't clean themselves.'

Mum of course. DIY and the cash to pay for it were Dad's priorities.

'You'll be doing plenty of overtime Gerry, if you're going to furnish this place. Can't sit on packing cases for ever. Let me know when you're ready for shelves, I'll be over to give you a hand.'

Dad meant well, but I wanted Gerry and our home to myself for a while.

Apart from the Rice family, the Stag and Pheasant and the Great Aunts in wartime, plus the few months in the Holland Park hostel, I'd lived with no-one other than my parents and definitely never with my peers. There were early misunderstandings, the first being our different habits at bedtime, especially after an evening out. I was happy to hang up my coat, clean my teeth and go straight to bed, while Gerry liked to wander round the house and perhaps stare out of the window for a while. I was upset because I thought he didn't fancy me, he because I rushed upstairs so quickly he thought I was avoiding him. Neither of us knew exactly how to broach this delicate topic. Talking openly about sex was still fairly taboo for us both and it was some weeks before we sorted that one out.

While I took for granted the societal norm that cooking and household chores were a wife's responsibility, it was sometimes difficult to conceal a slight resentment. We were both working full-time, yet Gerry could sit down and put on a record when he arrived home. I was the one who peeled potatoes before we left for the train and lit the gas under the saucepan each evening while the master sat with his feet up. I'd vowed not to be a nag like my own mother, but this would occasionally lead to a long silence on my part. Are pursed lips genetically inherited? Eventually he would ask
'What's the matter?'
'Nothing much.'
By the end of the evening I might have admitted to
'I wish you'd start cooking supper if you're home first.'
'Why couldn't you just ask me? I'm not a mind-reader.'
At least he didn't offer his mother as an example of the perfect housewife. After a few weeks his greeting on my 'pensive' evenings changed.
'I know there's nothing *much* wrong, but why not tell me now rather than waste the whole evening?'
A sensible suggestion – and it made me laugh.

Furnishing the house was fun, our tastes were similar and we spent most Thursday evenings in John Lewis or Heal's, when West End department stores stayed open until 7. Shopping was followed by supper in a Quality Inn, dining royally on rissoles (burgers) and chips, as second and even third cups of coffee came free. Friends recommended a small Greek café in St Giles High Street where we discovered moussaka, served with home-made coleslaw spooned onto our plates in vast quantities from a huge enamel washing up bowl. Aubergines were new to us and we ate there regularly until I'd worked out the recipe. It didn't occur to me to ask the chef.

The 'String' Swedish bookshelves we'd ordered were unusual, with sides and a magazine rack of black-coated metal bars rather than wood. Our next major purchase was a Swedish sideboard, with black and red doors and plain wooden top. IKEA is no trendsetter, young couples and design magazines in the fifties had already discovered Swedish furniture. As regular readers of 'House and Garden' we were offered monthly displays of tempting rooms, plus names like Ercol, G Plan, Robin Day, Gordon Russell. We might live in the suburbs but we aimed for Chelsea or Hampstead style.

Swedish bookshelves, TV and portrait of Lesley

We'd first been introduced to this type (and price) of furniture in Frederick Restall, a very upmarket furniture store opened in 1955 in Birmingham. Had Marjorie not insisted I'd never have had the courage to enter, despite frequently wandering round Heal's and Liberty's, London being more anonymous. Their wedding gift was easy chairs, but not just any old chairs. Marjorie insisted 'You must get them from Restall's, it's the only place.'
My choice was a G-Plan armchair in a kind of orange-rust (sounds awful, written like that but it was beautiful) and Gerry had a blue HK (Howard Keith). G Plan was originally Danish, so I was already halfway to following Scandinavian trends. Our kitchen cabinet, the sideboard and a delicate black chest of drawers were all from Restall's. The 2011 Exhibition at the Festival Hall which celebrated the Festival of Britain's 60th Anniversary left me nostalgic for our first home. The replica Fifties living room was familiar and I recognised our G-plan and Ercol furniture and Lucienne and Robin Day's curtains.

I was no artist but we had so much else in common, including many duplicated copies of books and records, though Gerry's collection included more jazz and opera, mine requiems and choral music and we enjoyed educating each other, listening as Gerry painted, with me or a friend as models.

By December, when I would be cooking my first Christmas dinner for our parents, we had six Italian dining chairs with rush seats imported by a new and promising designer, Terence Conran who later opened Habitat stores. Thanks to wedding gifts we had three linen table cloths with matching napkins, wine glasses galore, modern wooden-handled cutlery from Liberty's, black and white Denby casseroles and serving dishes and a wooden salad bowl, but no china apart from Gerry's ancient cracked bachelor plates and a few throw-outs from our parents.

The day before Christmas Eve we realised we had no cooking surfaces, fitted kitchens being a dream of the future, or for fatter wallets than ours. Gerry and Dad trawled local second-hand shops, returning with a bedroom cupboard minus its marble top, plus a sheet of hardboard from Dad's garage-cum-workshop. *Voila,* a kitchen cupboard plus worktop for less than £1. It served us well until we could afford our black cabinet, Swedish again, with its smoked glass doors and canary yellow Formica worktop. Formica was another new product. We now had twin guest beds too, used by us over the holiday while the parents-in-law slept in style in our bedroom with its Heal's curtains. The other bedrooms were curtain-less so we disrobed in the dark.

We'd known each other only as fellow actors until our first date in March, so this was my first Christmas with Gerry. I watched his delight in decorating the Christmas tree. His parents had been badly off when he was young, turkey and tree were bought when prices dropped late on Christmas Eve, so his first sight of the tree was on Christmas morning. He and Tony were evacuated during the war and recent Christmases had been spent in seaside hotels.
'When you're at work you can't be bothered with all the fuss,' Marjorie explained, 'You know I'm no cook. I always said my sons' wives would feed them better than I ever did. I was right, too.'

The sparkling tree and the heaps of parcels below it were magical. Christmas Day for me used to mean ancient paper chains, a few lights and cheap baubles on a small tree, then the perfunctory exchange of one parcel each before Mum retired to spend a martyred morning in the kitchen. I now discovered that no kitchen mayhem ensued as I joined the others to unwrap parcels.

I had no idea what to expect in the way of gifts from Gerry and was thrilled by his creativity and generosity. He made me close my eyes while he carried in from the hall a huge framed print of Picasso's 'Girl with a Dog.' A large glass chemist's jar stood beside it, filled with cooking chocolate in rocklike lumps whose colours matched many of Picasso's shades. Another soft parcel revealed an expensive and fashionable black fur beret which he'd made me try on 'as a joke' in John Lewis a couple of weeks earlier. I still treasure the picture; the glass jar, which for years held either chocolate or for an hour or so after they emerged from the oven, home-made biscuits, now stores soap in Suzy's bathroom.

I don't remember what anyone else bought, but there was an unexpected gift to come. My parents had left, Gerry and Gordon were washing up, Marjorie and I relaxing by the fire. She leaned towards me.

'Thank you for making him so happy. Tony thought you might not, it was all so quick and you are nothing like the last one.'

How many mothers-in-law offer such a tribute? Mine would have been more likely to commiserate with Gerry over my shortcomings.

TIME FOR BABIES

Working at the Colonial Office became far less interesting. I'd returned in November to a new post. Civil Service regulations stated that on marriage a woman could receive a Dowry of a month's salary for every year she'd worked, but she would be required to resign, with the right to return at a lower grade but no longer with pension rights. If, instead, she stayed in her current post a frozen pension would be available when she resigned. No-one doubted a woman's fecundity or wishes, and resignation would normally automatically follow motherhood, which might mean waiting another thirty years before the pension became viable. A lump sum of six months' untaxed salary was an obvious choice.

Gerry had saved enough for a deposit of £200, 10% of the £1975 price of our house, but we needed to furnish it and naturally intended to have a family. I was duly demoted to Clerical officer and for several months worked in the Registry, tracing and delivering files for former colleagues. A more sensitive organisation might have moved me to another department, even another building, but this may have been their way of ensuring staff would become unsettled and leave. I applied for and was shortlisted for several jobs, but my honest response to the inevitable
'I assume you will be starting a family?'
always ended the interview.

After almost a year I was finally accepted by the London County Council, though there was a minor problem about starting at County Hall. I was definitely pregnant. Pregnancies were confirmed only after two periods had been missed and at the job interview the interviewer had for once failed to state
'I expect you'll be starting a family soon,'
but it might not be a good idea to tell them on my first day that I would be staying for only a few months. The pregnancy was not exactly unexpected, but my periods had been erratic since I began a regular sex life. Dr Barrett would laugh at my regular visits to ask
'Have I made it yet?'
'Relax, don't be in such a rush. Unfamiliar activities are upsetting your hormones my dear.'
He'd known me since childhood, had refused me contraceptives until a week before the wedding and like most family doctors in the Fifties diplomatically assumed the 'activities' were unfamiliar.

I decided to bluff it out at work, pretend ignorance until I was forced to admit that my expanding waistline was not due to overeating, but I was exposed quite soon. The colleague who sat opposite me caught German measles from his children. I had never had it and my experience earlier in the summer had left me prone to panic. One of the older women in the office smiled knowingly and told me not to worry too much

'Fred probably stayed home in time and you don't use his cup. You're wondering how I guessed? I've had four, my dear, you get to recognise the signs.'

She was right, but the memory of the episode in Guernsey was still vivid. It was our first holiday abroad, if the Channel Islands where they spoke English and we didn't need passports, counted as abroad. I was a mere three weeks overdue, but this time it felt different. I planned to register on our return with a doctor in Eltham who might take me seriously, unlike Dr B.

On the train from Waterloo we chatted with a couple, Jo and Aubrey. Like us, they had booked at the Bungalow Hotel where their friends were already staying. They went for dinner; Gerry joined them but I was convinced I would be sick if I tried to eat. I'd rarely travelled by sea, certainly never been seasick, but I was taking no risks. Vomiting repulsed me. Gerry teased me if we met drunks on a late-night train, I was so nervous in case they threw up.

'You make more of a fuss than they do.'

We had not booked cabins, so slept on and off on benches in the lounge, waking early to the sound of heavy rain. We washed, drank coffee, found our new friends and prepared to land.

The gloomy expressions of the group waiting on the quay under umbrellas were due to more than the weather. We were introduced to Geoff, Anne, Julie and Peter and regaled with their complaints about the hotel, starting with the corrugated iron roof emphasising every raindrop and encompassing poorly cooked food, cramped rooms and miserable hosts. We were welcomed as allies in any official action, our holiday group established without effort and we remained friends for some years. The hotel was as ghastly as they'd said. Appalling food, plasterboard thin walls which might have put us off lovemaking had our badly sunburnt legs and backs not already put paid to that idea. The others made the week bearable, fun even, until the Thursday.

We took a boat to Herm for the day and I began to have appalling period pains, far worse than those which used to mean hours spent in the school sick bay. Back at the hotel, fortified by a double gin Julie assured me was purely medicinal, I went straight to bed. A couple of miserable days, then it was time to go home. The following week Marilyn Monroe's miscarriage generated vast publicity and I realised that I too had miscarried. We'd hired bikes, a possible contributory factor.

My childhood experience of both personal and family illness made me obstinately stoical over health issues and there was no way I was going to a doctor while we were on holiday. I'm not sure a doctor would have agreed this early that I was pregnant, so how could I miscarry? A month later I was certain I'd genuinely conceived and I joined a medical practice which we passed on our way to the train. The LCC interview was held three weeks before I could boast officially that I was expecting a baby.

Pregnancy wasn't the joyful experience I'd been promised. Horrific morning sickness for the first few weeks, until I discovered that coke fumes from the kitchen boiler were responsible for the worst bouts and kept away from it. It was an unreal, not-here-yet-might-not-even-get-born time. I'd had no experience of living with babies or small children, only with Grandmothers and Great Aunts but was determined to prove more loving than my own mother.

Three months after I left home Mum and Dad had acquired a TV. It was possibly the first time they'd been alone together in all the years they were married; the new interest seemed to me to provide a diversion from the poverty of their relationship. Mum developed what they called, to her fury, 'senile' diabetes. Medicine had advanced and she was fortunately able to inject herself. I could never have done what she did for Gran, not only the actual injections but we were living several miles apart.

One foggy evening in early December Gerry was out for the evening with Stan. I was listening to the radio while I ate supper when the programme was interrupted with news of a major train crash near Lewisham. I knew Gerry was safe but Lewisham was on Mum's route home. As we had no phone I asked to use a neighbour's. Dad hadn't heard the news and was irritated.
'Your Mum's late home. Don't know what's for dinner and I'm hungry.'
My stomach churned. Was she in the crash? Might she even be…?

'Did you know about the train crash? Ring the police, Dad and call me back on this number, I'm at Sylvia's. '

There was nothing any of us could do, the fog was far too thick for anyone to try to reach St johns and we would have been in the way. An hour so later Dad rang back.
'She's all right, four of them walked to Shooters Hill Police Station. They've given them drinks and grub and will bring her home. They said it's too foggy for me to drive.'
With Mum's diabetes I knew she must eat regularly.
'Thank God. Give her some sugar and make sure she goes straight to bed. Tell her I'll ring in the morning.'
Relieved but still anxious, before I went upstairs I left a note for Gerry to wake me whatever time he arrived home. Stupid, perhaps, but there was always the remote chance he had cancelled the outing and was on that train. He woke me well after midnight.

'Why the note? Absolute bloody chaos at Charing Cross, they took us to Woolwich. Had to get a taxi. Ridiculous, all because of a bit of fog.'
'But don't you know what's happened?'
To avoid panic the crash hadn't been mentioned at Charing Cross, there were simply apologies for the delays. Once he knew the scale of the disaster Gerry was mollified. Next morning our trains ran almost on time. Our coach was very quiet as we passed the mangled carriages hanging over the edge of the raised track at St Johns.
Mum was badly shocked both by what she'd seen and heard and by the long walk, though she confessed she'd enjoyed being fussed over by the police. The episode made me suddenly very conscious of my responsibility for the small creature moving around inside me. Having a phone installed became essential, our only option a party line, shared with another user who seemed to talk constantly, but better than no phone at all.

As the pregnancy advanced I became hugely protective, eating the right things, knitting, sewing, resting, doing all the exercises and practising the breathing, but there were worrying moments when we realized how having a baby would curtail some of our activities. We'd planned to buy bikes but would no longer be able to go out just whenever or wherever we chose, visit friends, theatres, cinemas. On the other hand Gerry enjoyed calling me by Julie's invented nickname, 'Pregnapotamus.' He would stroke, touch, pat the bump, try out boys' names. Boys again! He would heave me into bed, cut my toenails, help me climb out of the bath.

108

Morning sickness was followed by heartburn.
'That's your baby's hair tickling you,'
was the smirking comment of one nurse. Silly woman, Sean was born almost bald.
I fainted once on the train going to work. When he saw that someone made sure I had a seat, Gerry continued to read his paper. I excused it as shyness and hatred of scenes, but those friends I told were more caustic. There were further indignities. An iron deficiency meant injections in my behind, alternate buttocks every 48 hours and ungainly bus journeys home, it was impossible to allow the jabbed side to touch the seat.
My parents argued over the gender, toasting the 'bump' on my birthday
'Here's to my daughter's daughter' – Mum.
'Here's to my daughter's son' – Dad.
Nothing new there then.
I made maternity clothes, including a grey flannel suit with a scarlet lining, 'to wear afterwards.' No woman wears maternity clothes when she no longer resembles the side of a house, but I did put it away for next time, I was definitely not going to stop at one.

Antenatal classes were highly practical. The midwife, Mrs Boyd told us not to listen to anyone who said childbirth should be painless. 'What can this Grantly Dick-Read know - he's a man. Natural Childbirth Foundation indeed. Trust me, I've had four. And don't bother to try kneeling, back or side is most practical, girls. I can tell you that when you think you can't stand any more pain, that's when it will change and the pushing stage will begin. Then it's nearly over – and it's worth it.'
Some of us were still less than convinced of the latter, but we all knew it was too late to change our minds about giving birth. Mrs Boyd's predictions were spot on.

One bonus was the friends I made, especially Janet Stott. She and I would meet for lunch or stop to chat in shopping aisles, bulges almost touching, oblivious to other customers whose way our bulk barred, creating even worse barriers when joined by Barbara, a Polish sculptor living in one of the Span houses I still coveted.
I lumbered on the bus to greet Anne Kristin Stott the day Janet brought her home. She was a baby, nothing special. It seemed I was still somewhat ambivalent and anyway, I wanted a boy. Well, Gerry and my Dad wanted a boy and I was always anxious to

please my men.

'Perhaps she'll encourage yours,'
a proud but exhausted Janet beamed, but everyone knew first babies arrived late. Kristin had been due three weeks earlier. I still had ten days to go and if I followed Janet's example that meant at least another month.

That weekend Gerry decided he must finish building the wardrobe in the front bedroom, which entailed Pregnapotamus spending Sunday afternoon holding planks of wood above her head while he measured, then fitted them. That night I felt extra tired, but next morning my energy levels rose. I planted summer bulbs, changed the sheets, cooked a complicated meal. Around midnight I woke in a damp bed.

'Gerry, wake up. I think something's happening. Ouch.'
An excruciating pain left me bent as near double as I could manage. The speed with which Gerry reached the phone to call an ambulance would almost have qualified him for the Olympics. My bag had been packed for a week, thanks to Mrs Boyd. No time for a midnight cuppa, I shivered all the way to the hospital, a mixture of fear and exhilaration.

I was booked in to the British Hospital for Mothers and Babies in Woolwich, had paid my last visit only a week before, when the obstetrician Dr David Morris invited two of us, if we lasted out, to join him on a Third Programme talk. I was going to miss that opportunity. There were no delivery beds free and the ambulance was sent from the wonderful British Hospital to St Nicholas Hospital, Plumstead, where they shared some of the same staff. Gerry was ordered home once I'd been examined and my labour pains confirmed. I was left in a small room, alone. Nothing more happened apart from the odd twinge.

AND THEN WE WERE THREE

Overnight, I dozed and occasionally groaned. Gerry had a raging toothache when I was three months pregnant, an affliction fairly prevalent in expectant fathers. This time he developed **a** heavy cold. Was he competing? He rang the hospital at intervals next day, to be told I was doing well but slowly, which in translation meant the contractions had almost disappeared and I was some kind of fraud taking up precious space. At visiting time he arrived watery-eyed and sniffing, full of praise for my mother's Irish stew, which I always refused to cook as it reminded me too much of childhood battles over bones. He was however unwilling to listen to further doom-laden recitals of her own horrific labour.

'I'll eat at home from now on. Shan't starve. I've lined up tins in the hall – soup on one side, raspberries down the other,'

Next morning, contractions still only intermittent, I wandered around in the main ward talking to other mums, very shocked by one cheerful woman's tale.

'I knew my baby was dead before she was born but I had to give birth naturally.'

Why was she still here among all these live babies and why was she not heartbroken? Dr Taylor, my GP, later told me that the answer to my first question lay in the second. In denial, she had to stay in until she accepted that her baby had died. It still seemed brutal.

Around noon my waters burst properly and all hell was let loose. More than half a century ago yet I remember almost every minute, hear myself gasping

'I can't, I can't, I can't...'

and the midwives saying

'Yes you can, just a few more p-u-u-u-u-ushes.'

I'd had no time to wash my long, pony-tailed hair and I apologised profusely. The midwife said cheerfully

'You might have had far more to worry about on the hygiene front, my dear.'

I understood the implication; I'd been given an enema on arrival at the hospital.

There was no question of fathers being present in the labour ward.

'More trouble than they're worth'

I heard one of the midwives say.

'One more push, come on now, then a pause before

111

'I can see your baby's head.'
'I want to see it. There's a mirror in my bedside cupboard.'
The mirror came and I saw what looked like a pale hairy finger. The blonde boulder tearing me apart became worth fighting for. A grand finale and it was out.

Not it: HE. This magical small being. Slightly less magical noises followed, a new-born's fury at being severed from his warm, wet haven. Miniature fingers curled round mine as he lay on my chest while the cord was cut. Covered in what resembled cream cheese, white fingernails, no eyebrows, red marks on the back of his neck and his forehead, he was the most beautiful thing I'd ever seen.
'He's a little early,' they told me, 'That's why his eyebrows and fingernails aren't perfect yet. The birthmark will fade. Have you given him a name yet?'
A blue ribbon marked 'Sean D Smith' was taped to his wrist and he was taken to be washed and weighed, while I waited for stitches, all the misery forgotten apart from the discomfort of legs shackled inelegantly in stirrups while the Doctor had tea.
Tea? I hadn't even had lunch.
'May I have something to eat?'
Polite as ever. The nurse grinned in sympathy.
'I'll look in the kitchen, but it's almost visiting time.'
So what? Giving birth was exhausting and I'd missed not only lunch but supper too. I was starving!
All the nurse could find were two cream crackers.
'Can I ring your husband and ask him to bring you something?'
'No, and don't tell him I've finally delivered, I want to surprise him.'
Stiches completed I was restored to dignity in bed in my private room. Gerry walked in, his sore and reddened nose covered in foundation filched from my make-up shelf. I smiled as he attempted to conceal a slight impatience. I'd been hanging around for two days with no end product. Prepared for yet further lingering, he was greeted by a smug wife nestling a two-hour-old bundle in the crook of her arm. Shakespeare's birthday too, even more clever.

His expression changed, his suddenly enormous hands reaching clumsily for the blanket. I watched as he cradled the bundle, tiny fingers curling round one of his. He'd had his boy, I'd got it right.
'You're not possessive,' he said.
Why would I be? This was his baby too and I wanted us to share him. Taking photos was not allowed and anyway Gerry hadn't brought his camera. I feasted on the two apples I'd asked for the

previous evening, they went down a treat with the cream crackers. 'Better not kiss you' he joked, 'Can't draw attention to my make-up, they won't believe I'm father material.'
Such comments were not considered in poor taste, even among arty liberals like us with several gay friends.

Proud Dad!

Sheer joy, those first few hours. Then agony, threats of catheters, taps left gushing for encouragement, bedpans, gross indignity. I asked to be moved to the maternity Ward despite warnings that I would regret leaving my single room for the noisy main one, but I wanted to see other babies, to share with other mothers my misery at the difficulty of breastfeeding. A brutal nurse had said curtly 'Some can, some can't. Stop fussing.'
The same nurse had suggested in the middle of my first night there that I should keep quiet. I'd kept so quiet that I missed breakfast. Now I was a heroine of sorts among the staff, thanks to my having viewed the emerging head in the mirror.

I was duly moved; a sixteen-year-old in the next bed had neither visitors nor a baby. She feigned sleep, spoke to none of us. A nurse confided in a whisper
'She's not married and her parents won't visit. The baby's going for adoption.'
Keeping the girl in the ward seemed cruel, as awful as with the mother who'd been made to stay after giving birth to her dead baby. Leaving these women among all the live babies may have been hospital policy, but nothing convinced me it was either helpful or necessary.
There was a variety of views on breast-feeding. Ruth Kellas, with

whom I stayed friends, was forbidden by her husband even to think about such a disgusting practice. As said husband ran his fingers daily over a shelf too high for Ruth to reach, checking for dust, I wondered what other problems he might have. Another wondered if I would mind if my husband saw me breast-feeding.

'Of course not. Why would I?'

'I'm scared mine might go off me,' she said.

Three-day blues, hormonal and almost compulsory arrived, but I was prepared and had sympathised over other tear-soaked hankies. The ten days lasted a lifetime, we seemed to be prodded, lectured or form-filling every few minutes and I longed to go home for a rest. My lovely Dr Morris visited each new mother's bed. He recognised me, asked

'Do you know what caused the strawberry mark on your baby's neck?'

So he still considered me worth talking to, though I'd missed the Third Programme discussion.

'No. Will it fade?'

'Probably, it's where the stork carried him in its beak.'

He moved on, far more amused than I by his wit.

Apart from husbands, only close relatives were allowed to visit. Mum duly arrived, her first question

'Did you have instruments?'

What else did I expect? The instruments accompanying my own birth were part of family mythology.

'No, I had a baby.'

'You've always got an answer for everything.'

Except why she couldn't simply be happy for me.

Gerry and Dad came to take us home. Despite Dad's plea to hold his grandson, I handed Sean to Gerry to carry to the car. When we arrived home I offered Dad the bundle but Mum was down the steps in a flash. Without asking, she grabbed the baby. Watching Dad's expression, for the first time felt sorry for him; I wondered which parent had really wanted a boy. After ten days of hospital food Mum's roast was extra tasty. Sated, I fed Sean then put him, like a shining trophy, in his pram in the front garden, where he fell asleep almost immediately. Mum and Dad went home while Gerry and I spent the afternoon peering every few minutes into the pram, assuming the next feed would be around teatime.

But this demand-fed baby slept on. Dr Spock, whose 'Mother and Child Care' was the baby bible of the Fifties, advocated feeding on demand, but he had nothing to say about babies who made none. We ate supper and still the little one slept, so we 'helped' him wake by banging the pram over the doorstep. Three hours later he was still wide awake and screeching and I was sitting at the top of the stairs clutching the banister, matching his howls with my own, having no idea what might happen next. Where was the nurse who would soothe him, remove him, change his nappy, a task I'd done only once? Where was the Health Visitor who was supposed to come and teach me what to do? It may have been almost midnight on a Sunday, but I didn't care. I'd never been so frightened before, but we all survived.

The Health Visitor took five days to call, suggested a top-up bottle, smiled and deserted me. She was probably calm and sensible, but I thought her unfeeling and harsh. MY baby was going to be completely breastfed. I learned to be slightly less anxious, though I always half-expected the house to have burned down if we ever dared take an evening off. After the first few days all was well, apart from evenings rent with three-month colic and a violent reaction at twelve weeks to banana, his first solids, also offered on a Sunday. Again no Health Visitor to consult, it was Gerald who reassured me by phone that Sean wasn't dying from dysentery and told me to express milk, a horrendously slow task. Apart from these small glitches, time seemed to pass in a haze of contentment, watching this new human grow into a person.

We became close friends with the Stotts. Janet was my junior by six years but with four brothers and sisters she was very matter-of-fact about motherhood, offering practical comments like
'I wouldn't leave Kristin to cry for hours, but you can't be at their beck and call every second. Most babies survive the odd missed feed. Don't worry so much.'
This was the kind of advice I'd have welcomed from my mother, but for her the traumas of my own first few months, when missed feeds were life-threatening, must have made it impossible for her to accept the more casual attitudes of my generation. She fussed all the time, reminding me within a few minutes of any visit to change his nappy, bring up his wind, urging me not to spoil him by picking him up whenever he cried.

115

MOTHERHOOD IS FUN

A few days after I came home a woman I'd never met knocked at the door and asked
'What did you have?'
How had a complete stranger known I was pregnant? This was Val Earl, who lived a few doors down the road with her children, Jim who was two and Jess, a few months older than Sean. I walked past their windows only a couple of times a day in the few weeks after I left work. It is astonishing how mothers-to-be fail to realise that our bumps are pretty visible. Gerry and John, Val's husband, had much in common and the Earls became our lifelong friends.

Gerry's parents came to London to greet their first grandchild and over the summer Marjorie often came for the day, combining her visits with a going to the theatre and always bringing gifts. She was no gushing Granny, but the compliments she paid my mothering more than made up for a lack of gurgles over Sean.
'I'm not really interested in babies, I prefer it when they start talking,' she said almost as a kind of apology, but she seemed to me the perfect mother-in-law.
Babysitting and nappy changing were not popular with either grandmother, but both still had full-time jobs, Marjorie lived too far away and I was mostly too tired to long for evenings out. We did occasionally go to a film or play, but I could guarantee to fall asleep within half an hour. Gerry painted in the evenings once all was quiet. Test matches against the West Indies and tennis at Wimbledon provided an excellent excuse to rent a TV, rentals being more popular than buying. Who needed babysitters?

I soon got to know other young mums in Castlewood Drive and daytime social life centred round pushing our prams in the woods behind our houses, discussing sleepless nights, nappy rash, when to begin weaning and other fascinating intellectual aspects of our new roles. Occasionally we would leave the babies at each other's homes while we shopped. Few of us had cars or even drove, so we walked to the local shopping parade at the bottom of the hill or even caught a bus to Sainsbury's in Lewisham, which had recently opened as one of the first self-service shopping centres and was for a short time the largest in Europe.

It was unusual for new mothers to return to work and I was happy at home, enthralled by Sean's every new action. The first time he turned over, recognised his hands, touched his toes, tried to sit up. As for the first tooth, I hadn't realised how competitive we parents were, boasting about our lack of sleep or the amount of weekly weight gain, by baby, not mother.

Household chores were not overwhelming, dusting and vacuuming were not major preoccupations. Unlike, or possibly because of Mum I was no fan of constant cleaning. I had a boiler with a wringer attached for the daily nappy wash, but was a far from brilliant laundress and Sean had regular nappy rashes. More ammunition for Mum's nagging, with added disapproval from the Clinic!

I could read a book or prepare the evening meal while he slept, but I did hanker at times for slightly more stimulating conversations. Val's children suffered from asthma and eczema and she was rarely free for strolls or chats. Beth now had fairly regular theatre work, often in touring shows and Jo lived too far away for frequent visits, as travelling to Hampstead involved bus, train and tube.

Janet and I met at least weekly, pushing our prams between Eltham and Blackheath, which offered us plenty of exercise. To take up less space on the pavements we would often put Sean and Kristin end-to-end in Janet's large Silver Cross pram. Second-hand, possibly a family heirloom, it was similar to the one used by the Royal princesses. Both babies had fair curly hair and often wore similar blue outfits. One day a shop assistant asked which was born first.

'Kristin, the girl.'

'How long between them, then?'

'Eighteen days.'

Why did the assistant look so shocked? By the time we reached the end of the street we realised she'd assumed they were twins and was imagining the suffering of whichever of us was the mother. For weeks the anecdote was inflicted on everyone we met.

A warm summer meant we could spend days at Charlton Lido, familiarising the babies with the water and in September we spent a week in Swanage with the Stotts, renting a flat above a craft shop with a café which stayed open in the evenings, something rare in the London suburbs. We would feed the babies and put them in their cots, leaving windows open and taking with us a two-way alarm, while we sat in the café eating meals we hadn't had to cook, having persuaded our men that wives deserved a holiday too. Later in the evenings we played bridge, something else Gerry had taught me, and argued politics. From the craft shop we bought a driftwood sculpture we named Henry and fell in love with a huge Victorian triple wardrobe, which we bought for £12. Haulage to London cost more than the wardrobe and we had no idea how we would get it up the stairs in our small house. The haulage driver explained that it came to pieces and our collection of antique furniture had begun.

On our return from Swanage we set up the Stott-Smith Saturday Dining Club as Janet and I wanted to learn to cook properly. We may not have had cars, babysitters or spare cash but there was a surfeit of wedding gift cookware and hungry husbands as guinea pigs. They were enthusiastic and promised to wash up, an acceptable division of labour without loss of male dignity. International cooking was the latest trend and we chose a different country each time. My kitchen sported long strings of French garlic, delivered regularly by a bicycling Breton, in beret and striped shirt. On Stott Saturdays Gerry and I would push Sean to Blackheath, a half-hour walk no problem for young legs, though Shooters Hill occasionally left one of us puffing at the summit. We climbed an iron fire escape to their top floor flat, hauling the pram with us.

Sean normally slept through the evening; his only protests coming in the early hours back home after a night feed suffused with spices. Don't ever believe breast milk is pure and filtered; beware the horrors of a pink nappy if Mum has supped on borscht. Over dishes like Indonesian nasi goreng, German frankfurters and sauerkraut, (though we'd already eaten this at Schmidt's in Soho) or French boeuf bourguignon we would put to rights the capitalist world.
'Give everyone £20 a week,'
was John's Christian Socialist view. We were agnostics but I knew my Bible.
'What about the parable of the talents?'
Religion and politics were favourite topics.
Until Janet's out-of-wedlock pregnancy John had been training to be a Minister in the Congregational church. It was an all-male college, with no married students allowed on the course. They'd considered it immoral to stay unmarried simply to save John's college place. I never once heard Janet complain about having to leave Edinburgh University after her first year. John became a door-to-door encyclopaedia salesman to pay their rent, for which I much respected him. Gerry and I were even more convinced of the hypocrisy of the church, my convictions fuelled by my high church

upbringing ('high,' because it was on a hilltop, I'd reasoned as a child) and the prig Gordon I'd dated at L.S.E.

Kristin was walking by Christmas, Sean took another few months, but he began to crawl, mostly backwards. It amused us but he found it both puzzling and frustrating. Janet pointed out to Mum, who once wondered in her presence if Sean was not very bright, that all babies developed at different rates. It was not a competition. 'There are advantages,' she said, 'Kristin is far too adventurous and she's accident-prone. Sean can be left to play without constant screams which mean rushing to check for broken bones.'

Mum thought Janet 'too uppity.'

Until he graduated to a pushchair, she regularly took Sean for walks, complaining

'What do you mean, he isn't going to wear shoes until he can walk?' I was defensive.

'The Health Visitor agrees it's a good idea, makes their feet tough.'

'Well I'm not taking him out with bare feet. People will think you can't afford shoes. I'll buy him a pair.'

'Fine, but only if you get his feet measured. He has to have Clarks or Start-rite, and he'll only wear them when he's with you, so you might be wasting your money, their feet grow so quickly.'

Gerry agreed with me that it was important to continue to use my brain, however minimally. He brought home a book of Van Gogh's letters belonging to a colleague who spoke no French and encouraged me to translate it. Then he persuaded me to take the Mensa test. I passed with an IQ higher than I'd imagined, but was grilled at the interview stage by three extremely pompous men and decided it was not for me. Qualifying was enough but I didn't bother to tell Dad, I wasn't sure he'd care.

The outside world was haunted by fear. Since Hiroshima the USA, Russia and Britain had developed powerful atomic weapons, generating worldwide concern about possible totally destructive wars. The Campaign for Nuclear Disarmament was formed, its members wanting Britain to take the initiative and get rid of our nuclear weapons. The first march from Trafalgar Square to the Aldermaston Atomic Weapons Establishment took place at Easter 1958 on the day Janet was giving birth to Kristin and I was resting my bump, but together with the Earls, we took part in later marches, pushchairs and all.

Our first Christmas with a child was approaching and we were excited. It was to prove disastrous.

EXITS AND ENTRANCES

Each set of grandparents seemed determined to outdo the other with Christmas gifts for their first grandchild. On Christmas morning my parents presented Edward Bear, who soon staked his claim as best friend forever. Gerry's gave several colourful Spanish outfits, far more interesting than any boys' clothes in English shops. Once Gerry and Tony were off their hands Marjorie and Gordon had begun to travel, mainly package holidays to still unspoilt Spanish fishing villages like Magaluf and Benidorm. Sean, now sporting eight teeth, became the best-dressed baby in the street.

Dad was surprisingly quiet, I'd expected him to monopolise his beloved boy. On every visit his first move was to grab Sean and bump him, shrieking with delight, on his knee in 'Ride a Cock Horse,' but today he stayed in the background, refusing the traditional mid-morning mince pie and sherry. At lunchtime I'd hardly served the turkey when he pushed his plate aside and rushed upstairs. Mum was unsympathetic.
'Trust him to moan. Says his stomach hurts. Fuss over nothing.'
'Shouldn't you go and see if he's all right?'
Marjorie asked, but Dad came back into the room, ashen-faced.
'Think we'll have to go home. Not sure I'll be safe to drive for long, stomach's playing up.'
Mum, her day ruined, had little choice but to go home. .
'Can't be helped I suppose. You don't look too great. I'll see you all tomorrow.'
The atmosphere was slightly subdued for an hour or so, but with a giggling baby eager to chew cardboard and ribbons, we soon recovered our hilarity.

We were spending Boxing Day with my parents. Gerry's Mum was unashamed to boast that she'd not cooked a Christmas dinner since before the war.
'It was hotels by the sea once the boys were working. I'm the world's worst housewife,'
she told us. Mum's raised eyebrows indicated that she, of course, would spend the morning in the kitchen cooking another vast meal, roast beef this time. On arrival we were greeted with a scowl.
'George is in bed. Sit yourselves down. Margaret, put the baby down and come and make some coffee.'

In the kitchen she confided they'd hardly slept, she was now genuinely worried.

'I don't like to fetch the doctor out on a Bank Holiday. You go up and see what you think.'

In their bedroom, one glance at a face almost as white as the pillow and I knew exactly what I thought, but Dad still refused a doctor.

'I'll be all right, shan't get up today. Spot of indigestion – I've taken Alka Seltzer. Don't let Trixie fuss.'

Arguing seemed to cost him too much energy so I stopped. He seemed scared - of Mum's nagging? The cost of a doctor's visit?

'Where will you find a chemist open to get a prescription on Boxing Day? Leave it. I can go to the surgery tomorrow if I have to.'

Gerry, Mum and I took turns to visit the bedroom, but decided it was better to keep Sean downstairs. I was surprised Marjorie made no effort to help with the meal, nor did she go upstairs to see Dad. At teatime he mentioned her absence. When I told Marjorie he would like to see her she frowned, suggested we leave early and shook her head when I invited her to say 'Goodnight' to Dad.

'He'll be more comfortable without us all crowding round him.'

For once I didn't blame Mum's tight-lipped frown as she almost slammed the door on us. She'd been worried yet had worked hard with a poor response from her guests. Back at home I put Sean to bed, then came downstairs to find Marjorie in tears and Gerry looking miserable. She responded to my frown.

'If I'm invited out I'm not usually expected to help. And I hate sick rooms. I'll tell George I'm sorry next time we're down. I hate Gerald being cross with me.'

This was a side of her I'd never seen. I offered her a cup of tea and Gerry followed me into the kitchen.

'She always does this, you can see why we don't often tell her off. Took some courage but I thought she needed to know she'd upset your parents.'

So our much-anticipated Christmas ended miserably. Marjorie was very subdued as she drove off next morning, Gordon loyally stroking her arm, intent as usual on avoiding any conflict.

Two days later Dr Barrett sent Dad to Charing Cross hospital, where he was kept in for overnight tests. They discovered a badly infected ulcer and he stayed there, on bed-rest until he was well enough for an operation. He would phone me in the evenings, wanting details of Sean's progress, making light of his symptoms now he was receiving attention, joking about fellow patients. Visiting hours were restricted and I was still breast-feeding, so I relied on these brief conversations to convince me he was not particularly ill. The operation was on a Thursday, but there was no way a baby would be allowed on the Ward so I relied on Mum's reports. On Saturday I took a framed photo of Sean to put on Dad's bedside table, to help his recovery.

Seeing him was a huge shock, he seemed to have shrivelled, his cheeks sunken, voice a slurred whisper. He clutched my hand.

'They've found something, they aren't telling me'

His mother and his older sister Ethel had died of cancer. Nothing would persuade him this was a fairly small ulcer, which had now been removed. Was this why he'd been so scared to see a doctor? I wept silently; I'm certain he didn't notice the tears and he might anyway have been glad to know I cared. A nurse asked if I would like a cup of tea and took me to a side room. As I sipped she said 'You know, showing yourself up like that won't help your father. If you can't pull yourself together perhaps you shouldn't come again.'

Would no-one allow me to escape guilt, now added to my misery and anxiety? Mum shrugged when I told her.

'No point in tears. It's a nuisance, being expected to spend so much time here. I'm going back to work on Monday. He doesn't need me there all day.'

Surely she couldn't be so callous?

'When will he be coming home?' I asked

'No idea. I'll ask them tomorrow. I'll have to take more time off work once he comes out.'

Why wasn't Dad getting better? Perhaps he was right and there was something seriously wrong that the doctors wouldn't tell us. Mum went to the January Sales.

'He's asleep most of the time. Might as well make the most of being near the shops.'

'Aren't you worried that he's been kept in so long?'
I asked.

'They know what they're doing. And he won't want to keep traipsing back here once he's out.'

For people of Mum's generation and background doctors always knew best, but on Monday afternoon she rang me. She sounded frightened.

'They sent for me. He's got pneumonia. Can you come up?'

When Gerry arrived home I handed over Sean and left to join Mum for a three-hour vigil outside the curtained bed, where doctors were

doing their best. One of them emerged from behind the curtain.
'Would you like to see Mr Fairman?'
Mum demurred.
'You won't want to see him like that.'
I'm not sure I ever forgave her but I never publicly defied her. We
sat in a chilly silence. Ten minutes later the young doctor
reappeared, his face grim.
'I'm afraid he's gone. Give us a few minutes and you can see him.'
Gone.
Was that what happened, did people simply go? Go where?
When I was finally led behind the curtain I saw a much younger face
than the one I'd wept over a week earlier. This one was calm,
unlined, shaved.
'That's not my Dad,'
but it was, released at 54 from all his problems. I didn't cry; hadn't I
been told not to make a fuss? We were offered the usual cups of
tea and a suggestion that we left the administration and came back
next day. I rang Gerry to tell him. Our neighbour Arthur offered to
drive to the hospital to take Mum and me home.
My only memory of the journey is feeling angry, I have no idea if I
spoke to Mum or even to Arthur. Gerry was on the phone when we
arrived. He ended the conversation, put his arms round me, told us
his parents sent their love and sympathy and suggested we all went
to bed. It was now well past midnight, but sleep was elusive. Weird
thoughts whirled. How dared my father die when I had finally done
something to please him, given him his boy? Why hadn't I gone
behind the screen to see him?' Did he know I was there?

Next morning I left Sean with Val Earl while Mum and I went back to
the hospital to sign forms and collect Dad's few personal items. I
sensed intuitively that she would get rid of most of his possessions
as quickly as possible and asked if I could have his wristwatch to
keep for Sean. I also managed later to retrieve our Christmas gift, a
metal toolbox Gerry had engraved with Dad's initials and which Dad
had never even opened.
Mum asked me to organise the funeral, my first ever, from our
house and prepare the funeral tea. More instruction than request
and from habit I agreed. Marjorie came down for the funeral. In
some kind of daze I handed round plates of sandwiches, cakes and
trays of tea to family, workmates and their few friends. I was
disgusted and alarmed when I overheard Mum and Marjorie talking.
'You won't bother marrying again, will you?'
'Good Lord no, once was enough. And Gerry says I can stay here.'

I buttonholed Gerry, demanding to know exactly what promises he'd made. Her husband buried only a few hours and Mum had her new life mapped out. I noticed she'd carefully charged Gerry with the invitation; there was no way I would have offered.

'Of course I didn't, I just meant for a few days. It seemed mean to send her home to an empty house when you both came back from the hospital. She must have misunderstood.'

Not the word I would have used. I wasn't totally heartless but I needed a break from the 'grieving widow.' She'd had few good words to say about, or to, Dad for years and now this wonderful husband was in her phrase 'taken from me.' The strained atmosphere lasted for three weeks until she returned home to sort out the mess – her words again.

I was so glad to have the house to ourselves again I assumed we would carry on as normal, except for seeing more of Mum at weekends and generally being supportive. Not so, I was expected to go regularly to Bexleyheath to help with jobs ranging from clearing out cupboards to major decorating, even though it entailed a complex journey by bus and train with a restless toddler. A couple of times Mum forgot to leave a key, not trusting me with one of my own. We would hang around in the garden waiting for her to arrive home from work, greeting us with amusement but no apology.

On Sean's first birthday I invited Jim and Jess Earl, Kristin Stott and their mums to tea. Gerry and Mum took the afternoon off and after the party was over we had

'What a pity Dad wasn't here – he always wanted a boy.'

'Really? I had no idea.'

'No need to be sarcastic.'

Then she began to cry. I'd had enough and slammed out of the room. My turn for tears, the first time since Dad died, including his funeral. When I came downstairs Mum had left, but I didn't care. For weeks I'd been irritable, had headaches, a rash, was sleeping badly. Gerry persuaded me to see Dr Taylor, who after the first few questions asked

'Had any shocks recently?'

'My Dad died in the New Year but I've got over it.'

'Takes a little longer than that, my dear.'

A long chat followed, plus a prescription for anti-depressants and a warning to be careful never to have my mother living with us. If only I had listened.

In June we went with the Stotts to the Private View at the Royal Academy Summer Exhibition; they'd been invited by John Bratby, an up and coming artist living in Blackheath whose wife, Jean, had been part of our NCT group, though sadly her baby was stillborn. It may have been the champagne, but Janet and I decided to synchronise our next pregnancies. I can't remember if we discussed it with our husbands, but it worked and our second babies were due in February.

We invited Mum to join us for a week in Birchington, near Herne Bay. The hotel provided evening card games and entertainment and we hoped Mum would offer us at least one evening off to spend by ourselves. In vain, we were expected to sit in the lounge with her, watching mediocre cabaret. One night Sean woke, wanting to play with his noisiest Matchbox cars. We took him for a moonlit stroll along the beach and he fell asleep, only to wake gleefully as we very carefully lifted his pushchair into the bedroom. At breakfast I was forced to beg Mum to look after him while we snatched a couple of hours sleep. She reluctantly agreed, but left me certain that his wakeful energy was down to my poor mothering.

The day after our return home I succumbed to a stomach bug, no fun when you are three months pregnant. Gerry caught the bug and we spent a day taking turns to cope with an energetic toddler and clutching our stomachs. I finally gave in and rang Mum, who was still on holiday. She appeared, calling up the stairs as she stepped in the front door
'No kettle on then?'
A brief hover near our bedroom door was enough to convince her we really were ill. I persuaded her to give Sean his tea, but nappy changing was out of the question and she left with a weak excuse, determined to avoid infection. I was wickedly pleased when she rang two days later to say she too was ill. Furious with her lack of care for us, Gerry said
'Don't you dare go over and look after her.'
Without his injunction I probably would have played dutiful daughter.

This pregnancy was far worse than the first, I developed bad varicose veins and was ordered bed rest, so simple to organise with a toddler around. By Christmas I was exhausted and we thought we might spend Christmas Day quietly alone with Sean. Mum had been invited to go to her brother Charles, but it would be her first Christmas alone and she begged to come to us. I realised I'd been

a little insensitive and for once gladly agreed to her request. Gerry's family was surprisingly demanding, Marjorie announced they would be coming for Boxing Day, 'they' including Tony and his wife. Tony and Liz were not my favourite people as they often phoned to say they were in London and were coming to stay the night, never asking if it was convenient. I said they could all come for Boxing Day if Gerry would book a restaurant for lunch, but somehow I ended up cooking, in danger of wearing a martyr's crown. Marjorie loved having her family together, but this time I was glad when they left. It had been difficult to stay civil when Sean climbed the stairs to jump on me while I was supposedly resting. I called down
'Please come and get Sean, I'm trying to sleep.'
'Do stop moaning,'
Gerry snapped. He was always unsympathetic in front of his family, possibly afraid of being thought henpecked, like his father.

In 1960 all babies, apart from the first, were born at home unless there were likely to be problems with the birth or the home was totally unsuitable. A midwife came a few weeks before the due date to inspect the bedroom we planned to use.
'You need a few bricks under this bed my dear. Ring me as soon as you're getting proper contractions.'
Proper contractions? How was I supposed to recognise improper ones? I found out. For at least a fortnight, usually late in the evening a few serious pains would convince me labour had begun, only to disappear as soon as I'd filled a hot water bottle and considered ringing the midwife. Mum came to dinner on my birthday, watching my every wriggle.
'Are you all right?' she asked more than once, 'didn't you say it was due today?'
My discomfort was due simply to backache but I teased her.
'So they tell me. How would you like to deliver a baby?'
She quite definitely wouldn't and left as soon as the plates were removed, without offering to wash up.

Five days later Gerry announced that it was as good a time as any for me to deliver, as he'd finished a project and could take a few days off without disruptions at work. Eager as I was to please, I doubted if I could oblige, but as we went upstairs to bed I realised the 'lump' was much lower than usual, my backache more pronounced. February was at its wintry worst, the streets chilled with ice and impacted snow. As a precaution I rang the midwife.
'I'm not sure I'm in labour but...'

I described my symptoms, heard a distinct sigh.

'I'd better come and look at you. I've been up four nights this week, the cold weather flushes them out.'

Once again I obliged with the girl we wanted. In less than two hours Suzy arrived, with Gerry there to hold my hand.

'It looks harder than I thought' he said.

'They are lying about painless childbirth,'

I managed. It was easier than the first time, but I wasn't prepared to admit that, I was enjoying the sympathy. Sean woke while I was in labour and Gerry went to comfort him. There was no way the midwife would allow a toddler in the room, apart from anything else we were all too busy, but I hated hearing him so distressed.

Suzy had a lusty cry, a mass of black hair and looked very like Dad. Gerry held her even sooner than he'd held his firstborn, but was less keen on the next step, assisting the midwife by disposing of the placenta. As a precaution, Dr Taylor came to check if I needed stitches. He reported

'I was stopped for speeding, but I said I was on my way to an urgent birth. The officer said "God Save the Queen" and waved me on.'

It was probably an apocryphal story, but Prince Andrew's arrival was imminent so I couldn't be sure.

'We should put an announcement on the garage door,' I giggled, before inelegantly failing to keep down my post-birth cuppa.

At his normal ungodly 6.30 a.m. Sean rushed into the bedroom to ferret in the Carrycot for the gift the baby had brought with her, a large bandy-legged and flexible giraffe, a Christmas gift we'd wisely kept in reserve. He and Gerry went to phone the grandparents. Not yet two but he was an early talker.

'Hello Gan-gan, baby girl. My got a giraffe in my tummy.'

Both Grandmas declared themselves shocked that we had begun Sean's sex education so early.

Uncle Charles asked if we would consider Georgina as a second name, to keep Dad's memory alive. We hadn't thought of it, but compromised with Georgette, though with hindsight Georgia might have been a better choice.

This time my mother knew better than to enquire about instruments, though she did comment

'Now you've got a pigeon pair, I hope you'll stop.'

I wasn't sure whether 'stop' applied to having babies or sex and certainly wasn't going to ask.

A VAGUE DISCONTENT

It was common after home births to be allocated a Home Help for a fortnight, to help with housework, laundry and childcare, paid for out of a Maternity grant for home confinements, I think around 3 shillings (15p) an hour. Mine admitted she preferred ironing to looking after toddlers, proving it by ironing even nappies and towels to avoid giving Sean any attention, but at least the house was tidy for a while. Our conversations would be along the lines of
'You've got a lot of books. They're all very well, but they do take a lot of dusting.'
Really? First I'd heard! Sean spent most of the next couple of days crawling over me, attempting to pull me out of bed. Gerry, convinced I'd thoughtfully delayed the birth for his convenience took a few days off work. He was happy to play with his adored son and also produced surprisingly edible meals, a practice he abandoned immediately I was allowed downstairs. Fortunately, though I'd given Mrs Kitchen, my once a week cleaning lady, time off she came to welcome the newcomer and took Sean out, complete with bendy giraffe who for a few weeks replaced Edward Bear. Home was a far more relaxing place than hospital to give birth, neighbours dropped in, sat on my bed, the midwife came daily to check that all was well, I could even snatch the occasional nap.

Third-day Blues were not confined to maternity wards; I was weepy, wanted visitors to go home, then felt rejected when they thoughtfully left me alone. The midwife's inspection over, the baby fed and safely asleep I was feeling sorry for myself. I suggested tentatively – no, I whinged - that I could do without Sean for an hour or so. Gerry was happy to escape, first providing me with coffee and The Guardian. Polly Toynbee was a young and exciting journalist and Mary Stott the editor of the Women's Page, aimed at women who could think, focussing on issues of interest to us beyond beauty tips and recipes. That morning Betty Jerman's article, 'Squeezed in Like Sardines in Suburbia' compounded my misery. Based on her own experience as the mother of young children, she wrote:
Home and childminding can have a blunting effect on a woman's mind. Many of them look back with regret to the days they spent in an office. Their work kept them alert.'

I recognised something of myself. With two children it could only get worse, I would become a suburban sardine, boring myself and everyone else. What had made me think I wanted a family? One

glance at my children and I knew. A few days later, once I was up and about and 'resting' a distant memory, I read a letter on the Women's Page. Maureen Nicol asked how, when a husband's job meant constant house moves, did she make women friends other than at the school gate or the clinic? Five-minute chats were no guide to the possibility of introducing topics beyond the price of cabbages or the best way to cure nappy rash. The letter ended
'Perhaps housebound wives with a desire to remain individuals could form a national register.'
It was as if her letter were addressed to me personally.

Conversational and even culinary skills were rapidly disappearing; opening a book a sure signal for sleep. I did have the extravagance, with two little ones in nappies, of a nappy service. This entailed leaving on the front doorstep each night a pail full of nappies needing attention, to be exchanged next morning by another pail full of exquisitely soft white nappies – bliss for us all!
My neighbours were delightful women whose babies, like mine, cried and made demands and who, also like me often felt like a combination of milk bar and servant, but I never seemed to fit in. It would have been patronising and possibly alienating to have asked as we pushed our prams if they'd enjoyed last night's Shakespeare on TV. One day we discussed a report in the tabloids that the Queen washed her own nappies, wondering if it could possibly be true…
Val was different but as Jim and Jess were often ill with asthma and eczema she was preoccupied and exhausted and rarely joined our walks. Janet and I saw each other less frequently now we each had a toddler and a baby to push in heavy prams.

Gerry took for granted our discussion of Guardian articles and books after dinner and he decided night feeds offered an opportunity for me to read more Proust. I failed miserably, nodding over the book propped opposite my guzzling baby and I never got beyond Volume 2 of 'Swann's Way,' which I'd begun during Sean's night feeds. Still haven't. Gerry read all twelve volumes on rush-hour trains, followed by Gibbons' 'Decline and Fall of the Roman Empire,' but he was hardly the archetypal suburban man.
Together with hundreds of others I replied to Maureen's letter.

Everyday routine took over and I forgot the letters. When Suzy was six weeks old I had a bad attack of bronchitis. As I wept and coughed in the early hours I would rock her, then put her downstairs in her pram, as far away from the bedroom as possible, so I could pretend

she wasn't there and try to sleep. She was probably hungry but it never occurred to me that breastfeeding might not be satisfying her. To my eternal shame, at breaking point one night I shook her. Her screams woke Gerry and I remember him taking her from me and saying quietly
'Go back to bed.'
When he returned to bed the house was silent apart from my sobbing. I have no idea what he did to calm the baby, we had no bottles in the house, but perhaps my anxiety had made her worse. He refused to let me talk about it.
'Wake me next time you feel that desperate. And see Dr Taylor about that cough.'

I was never again tempted to harm one of the children, but the episode helped me to understand how terrifying my mother must have found my first few months. Except that there was never a time I didn't want any of my children and these early crises passed. Suzy slept quietly during the day, but she got her own back eighteen months later. The first time she slept through the night was the day we moved house. We were woken not by a rattling cot and yells for 'Mummy,' but by the removal men at the door!

Maureen Nicol contacted me and we met when she visited London. She'd had more than a hundred letters from London alone and invited me to be London Organiser of the newly-formed National Register of Liberal-minded Housebound Wives, which to some extent saved my sanity, though the mouthful of a title became an encumbrance. At a summer party in Blackheath one of the male guests, a very dishy psychiatrist, asked me to dance. Gerry (joking, I think...) warned me to behave – as if 1961 was pre-Women's Lib.
A rather odd conversation accompanied my chaste waltz with D.
'Do you have problems in getting out?'
'No, we're lucky, my Mother baby-sits.'
'Yes, but is it difficult, do your hands get clammy, do you feel shaky?'
He nodded at a couple, the man's hands stroking his wife's bottom
'That's what it's about, you know, sex.'
I was bemused, then collapsed into giggles. He'd assumed any housebound wives were agoraphobic. I put him right and he avoided me for the rest of the evening.
Not long after, the name was changed to 'The Housewives Register,' although I'm not sure how much my encounter influenced this.
Our group stayed small, its members from Eltham, Plumstead and Blackheath. We met during the day with our children, some of us

becoming close friends. There were also evening discussions of fairly rigorous topics, among them the novels of Iris Murdoch and L P Hartley; 'Culture and Society'; 'Unnatural death (suicide, euthanasia, abortion)' and 'Communal Living.'

Press and TV interviews followed some, like the Sunday Times and the Daily Telegraph, more positive than others. The Evening News sent a female reporter. I farmed out Sean to Val and Suzy was asleep in her pram in the garden. Uninvited, the woman followed me into the kitchen while I made tea. There was a neat pile of clean baby clothes on the worktop and two Matchbox cars on the living room carpet. Later Mum rang, mortified that I had not tidied the house.
'But of course I did.'
Gerry brought the newspaper home. Halfway down the column I read 'The kitchen was festooned with nappies and toys littered the carpet.' Then Alan Whicker headlined us 'Miserable Married Women.' It was the last time I trusted a journalist.

The first months with two babies were exhausting. Sean was an energetic toddler and his potty-training had been at best half-hearted. Disposable nappies were still a rarity but I did get a proper washing machine. A malfunctioning milk bar-cum-launderette, I probably had mild post-natal depression, though I'm not sure it was a recognised condition. Janet seemed to cope with Mark easily enough, which naturally left me feeling, as usual, a failure. Gerry would come home from work and take Sean off for his bath and 'Jumps on bed,' a hilarious game they played. I think I resented their untroubled relationship, plus the fact that at that early stage there was little he could do to help with Suzy. I began to feel that Sean preferred his Daddy, as well he might, Mummy was always occupied during the day with this baby who couldn't play with him. Once I caught him posting coins from his money box down her throat as she lay on the carpet.
'We were playing postman,'
he explained. Fortunately she seemed not to have swallowed any.

In August we rented a cottage in Dymchurch, where I was grateful for leisure time asleep on the beach or in the garden while Gerry played with the children. We managed to block the toilet with the disposable nappies we were using as a holiday treat for me. The cottage owner was not amused. Gerry cooked on alternate nights and attempted to teach Sean the rudiments of cricket, as the Earls were staying nearby and John and Jim sort of played Gerry and Sean on the beach.

Dymchurch, Summer 1960

Suzy's persistence and patience were clear from early days. She walked before her first birthday but talked much more gradually than Sean. He burbled gibberish, which I swore I understood, from about nine months and was highly articulate by the time he was two, but Suzy refused to use a word until she could say it properly. She would observe and copy Sean all the time, desperate to manage everything he could do, potty-training herself at sixteen months, although she found being unable to stand properly at the toilet highly disappointing. Gerry and I once timed her for half an hour as she assembled a pile of small objects she was determined to carry across the room in one load. Each time she dropped one she began again, engrossed, uncomplaining - and she DID it.

One day she took herself for a walk down the road. We had mistakenly considered our house safe as the steps were too steep for small children to climb. Most small children. Suzy was adventurous. Fortunately a neighbour brought her home before I'd missed her. Gerry built a two-storey Wendy house in the garden with windows which opened and the children spent hours playing at ice-cream vans, shops, the Three Bears and invented games. There was a sandpit too, small feet trampling as much sand into the house as the garden.

By the end of its first year the London Housewives Register had four organisers. I took part in an afternoon TV programme hosted by Elaine Grand, a Canadian presenter. Over sandwiches and one very small glass of sherry we were briefed on likely questions before the programme. This was a period when afternoon TV offered intelligent discussions, good plays, cookery programmes with chefs like Robert

Carrier and Fanny Craddock presenting meals the average housewife might both cook and afford. I came home with a cheque for £8 (one-third of Gerry's weekly salary) and an ambition to be a TV presenter. A flattering phone call from Claire Rayner, TV personality and agony aunt, convinced me it would be only a matter of weeks before I was offered a contract. I was put in my place when the neighbour who'd looked after the children for the day said
'We asked the kids to shut up while the programme was on but they said it was only Sean's mum!'

Vanity… but it did get me dinner with Gerald Sanctuary of the Marriage Guidance Council, forerunner of Relate, who admitted he visualised the Register rather as a body of prospective social workers. He accepted somewhat grudgingly my explanation that most of us were too busy to take on more commitments but felt we had a right to a self-help group. He invited me to train as a marriage counsellor, not quite the call to fame I'd envisaged.

This was the decade of pressure groups; any organisation originating in The Guardian was guaranteed to have members involved in issues like the Campaign for the Advancement of State Education, CND, anti-capital punishment. I met Belle Tutaev and we supported her campaign for Pre-School Playgroups.

My brain slowly resurfaced and I joined a Writers Course at Goldsmiths College. Ambition returned when the tutor suggested I send one of my stories to 'Listen with Mother,' but I did nothing with it. Mum came over occasionally to babysit while we went to the theatre or a film and we made another visit to Glyndebourne, Cosi Fan Tutte this time. We had to leave the house at lunchtime so Gerry's parents came to stay.
The Saturday dinner club was no longer, but was succeeded by Sunday lunches, the cuisine slightly less haute and the conversation very disrupted, more for the women, the men developing intermittent deafness to children's demands.
Our next problem was space.

PUTTING DOWN DEEPER ROOTS

There were daily reminders of the limitations of a full length living room, rather than separate dining and sitting areas with walls between and at least one room civilised. The kitchen, though long, was too narrow to squeeze in a table or even a newly fashionable breakfast bar. Every evening I tidied toys, crumbs and clutter before Gerry came home. By the time the children were in bed and we'd eaten I was, in Gerry's words
'Too exhausted to be fun.'
Helping on the house was not a requirement for husbands who, unlike mere mothers, had been working hard all day.

We decided to move to a larger and less conventional house. Artists, even those with a day job, shouldn't be confined in a dormitory suburb. Our half-formed plan was to find somewhere more rural. Gerry's colleague Doug lived near Epping and encouraged us to move there. John Stott's church had moved him to Ilford so, apart from occasional treks, I'd lost Janet. Ilford looked even duller than Eltham and was hardly rural, but after a Sunday spent with Doug and Heather, with lunch at a country pub and a walk in Epping Forest, Essex was added to our list alongside Kent. Journeys to view properties, most of them totally unsuitable, took up most of our weekends. Hours on trains with two small infants were exhausting and our friends Norman and Cherry Bryce offered to drive us all one evening to Faversham. The house was beautiful but impractical, with a noisy timber yard next door, possibly the owners' motive for leaving, and a tiny garden, plus long and expensive commuter train journeys for Gerry which would leave him even less time for painting.
'Why are you looking so far out?' Norman asked as we piled back into the car with two sleepy children. 'Delayed adolescent rebellion? Dreams of self-sufficiency? Forget it. Stay in London.'
As she got into the car Cherry trapped a finger in the door and we discovered that the nearest hospital was several miles away. This was the deciding factor. We had other viewings booked but were ready to agree with Norman.

There was also Mum to consider. Still very needy, she'd be even more demanding if we moved miles away. I'd read an article about a new venture, a block of privately owned flats for older people in Worthing, one of her favourite holiday settings. Somewhat unrealistically, I suggested she might consider moving there, thinking we would have a seaside retreat and the children could spend holidays with her as they grew older

I ought to have known better, she chose to interpret it as wanting to get rid of her. Not a conscious motive, but who knows?

Our plans to move had been kept quiet; but once I revealed them Mum began to drop heavy hints about buying a big house to share. We were certainly tempted by the capital she would invest, but Gerry completely failed to understand my qualms. He adored his own mother, who could do almost no wrong and soothed me, promising to make quite sure Mum lived in a separate Granny flat.

Tiring of these trips we cancelled a viewing of a house in Billericay to spend Easter in Birmingham, where Marjorie tried to warn Gerry.

'I wouldn't dream of inflicting myself on any of you. And if I go first, don't take Gordon in, he'd drive you mad. Trixie is even worse. She'd nag Margaret day and night, make her life a misery.'

Someone on my side, then, but unfortunately Gerry for once refused to be influenced by her, his sights now set on living in the more arty Blackheath/Greenwich area. He had joined the Blackheath Art Society and had already made new friends. Without Mum's help we would never raise enough cash to move to this more expensive area. We had to begin thinking about the children's education too. Sean was three and if we stayed would soon be eligible for the nursery class at Deansfield, the local primary school. It wouldn't be fair for him to start there and then suffer a double uprooting.

Mum put the Gipsy Road house on the market and found a buyer within weeks. She sold some of her furniture, stored the rest and spent the summer lodging with a colleague in Croydon. It offered companionship for her, but it must have been difficult for both of them, being together both at work and home. Mum spent most weekends with us, on her best behaviour, helping with the children and complimenting me on my cooking, though not on my tidiness or housework. I began to convince myself the future might be bearable, especially if she had her own self-contained flat.

We found a sprawling Victorian house in Lee Green, not quite Blackheath and therefore affordable. Unfortunately the house needed a vast amount of work, especially as we planned to convert part of it to a Granny flat. We were refused a mortgage, which created a major problem. Buying outright would have cleared our capital and most of my mother's. Our early upbringing left us too unsophisticated, or possibly scared, to take out a huge loan. Mortgages were more legitimate, somehow they didn't count as loans. One of the main attractions of the house was its remnants of Victoriana. A baize-covered door leading into the kitchen area, a vast walk-in pantry, a framed case of brass bells high on the kitchen wall, to summon a maid to every room. No longer either working or necessary, but covetable. There was a Welsh dresser full of china, huge meat dishes, cast-iron cauldrons for cooking gargantuan stews, canteens of silver cutlery. The vendors were uncaring and obviously philistine relatives of the owner, an elderly, recently dead recluse. We could almost have set up as antique dealers, had we not wanted to keep most of it. Perhaps we had a lucky escape. Within two years a block of new houses was built so close to the house that we would no longer have been able to see out of the side windows.

Disappointment was forgotten when we saw a house in Coleraine Road, Greenwich, especially when the next-door neighbour Gabi Marston, who later became a good friend and part of the primary school car pool, invited us in for coffee. We made an offer, put Castlewood Drive on the market and asked John Earl, who was a senior surveyor in the L.C.C.'s Historic Buildings Department, to survey Coleraine Road. He pronounced it almost perfect. Two days later we were told the original buyer had offered more – we had been used as bait for a higher bid.

When we'd bought the Eltham house it was still only a paper plan, so we had no idea how horrible a process selling would be. People were openly critical in my hearing, possibly hoping for a reduction in price but only making me determined not to sell to them. Comments like
'I couldn't bear to live with these awful purple curtains,'
tempted me to reply
'Don't worry, I'm not selling to you so you won't have to.'
We accepted an offer from a family who came along twice to measure for carpets and various appliances, then without explanation withdrew their offer. Gloom and despair as we wondered if we were doomed to live forever in Eltham.

Then we found 12 Vanbrugh Hill, a four-storey Victorian villa near Greenwich Park which included a separate semi-basement flat. Couldn't be better, Mum would be living with us as she wanted but we would each have our own front door. There were five bedrooms, one of those on the top floor earmarked immediately for Gerry's studio. No more reek of oil paints in the living room, or keeping wet canvases out of the children's reach. The owners, a naval family leaving a post at the Royal Naval College, wanted a quick sale and at £5,500 it was affordable. Selling Castlewood Drive became urgent but there were few serious viewers.

Until the Friday call from the estate agent.

'A viewing for you, couple in a hurry. They'll be there in fifteen minutes. No problem, I hope.'

No problem? Ann Caldwell, Fiona (6), Richard (3) and Jeremy (6 months) were spending the day with us. Four small children playing shops, or buses, or whatever necessitated a row of chairs running the length of the living room. Half-full beakers of juice, some of their contents mingling with biscuit crumbs on the floor, dirty lunch dishes piled on kitchen surfaces, a yelling Jeremy refusing to settle for a nap. Panic-stricken, I remembered Friday was sheet-changing day. All the beds were stripped but not made up. Where to start, or should I just call back to cancel? They were probably already halfway here. Ann and I rushed upstairs, concealed the mattresses and pillows with coverlets. There was no time to tidy the kitchen or corral the kids before the ring at the doorbell. The wife smiled politely, insisting that the untidiness was not a problem, but I didn't believe her. Their viewing was scarcely more than cursory.

When they'd gone Ann and I collapsed on the nearest available chairs, ignoring protests that we were sitting in the bus driver's seat.

'Never mind,' she soothed me, 'Can't win 'em all.'

Half an hour later the agent rang.

'You must have made it look good, they've made an offer.'

Oh, yes, the house had been immaculate.

'I advise you to accept. They want a quick move so you need to hurry your end. They loved the quirky floor tiles.'

I was surprised they'd been able to see any tiles under the toys and gunk. Gerry was delighted but cautious. I didn't blame him, but they remained buyers, waiting until contracts were exchanged before their next visit, refusing my apologies for the original chaos. The wife said

'I was one of six kids, I liked the atmosphere. And these colourful floors. My husband's the practical one but he's happy too.'

I was already planning to set up a business renting out rowdy small children to other despondent sellers. We dared to be optimistic, made plans for our new home.

Two weeks before the move, Mum delivered her blow.

'Please don't make me live in that basement. It's dark and a bit damp. You aren't going to charge me rent, so you could make some money there if you rent it out.'

Gerry looked shocked but left me to plead our case.

'But you'll need a kitchen and there's only one bathroom.'

'You've plenty of spare rooms. Gerry doesn't need a whole bedroom just to paint in.'

That roused him.

 'Actually I do. And where...?'

She'd spent time thinking this through, guessed what he would say next 'The front bedroom has that room off it. I'll pay to have a kitchen put in.' Money again; bribe or blackmail? Would I ever learn to stick up for myself? I was more than furious, I felt defeated and manipulated. Her considerable financial contribution to the purchase, though rarely mentioned was always implicit. Gerry hated direct confrontation and was impressed by the notion that rent from the basement flat would cover the mortgage, which was to be £65 quarterly.

So I gave in with suppressed fury, mostly with myself for my cowardice, but without further argument. Our space already minimised, our privacy threatened even before we moved in. The main bedroom, with a dressing room attached, became Mum's living room and kitchen. I did insist that her bedroom was on the top floor, next to Gerry's studio and the attics, there was no way I would allow her to sleep in a room near us. That left two rooms on the first floor, one a bedroom for us, the other for Sean and Suzy, who now had to share. Not what we had planned. We now had a five-bedroomed house but still no guest room and only one bathroom for five of us. We would be putting a spare bed in the studio, but could hardly ask Gerry's family to sleep with lingering smells of paint and turps, nor with sketches which would probably be strewn around once there was no urgent need to clear up after an evening's work. They would still have to stay in hotels when they visited. Was my refusal to stand up to my mother pathetic, or inevitable?

A further crisis threatened our moving date, fixed for a Monday in October. On the preceding Friday, an hour before his office closed, our solicitor rang to say the local Fire Officer was insisting that all internal doors must be fireproofed, as the basement was a separately rated dwelling. The previous owners, already living in Bath, were legally responsible but the solicitor had been notified only that afternoon. Or had he failed to notice the requirement until he glanced at our file before leaving for the weekend?

I wondered if anyone ever moved house without major traumas. If panic and disappointment were inevitable, why put oneself through such hell? On Monday the removal van would appear, gas, electricity and phone would be disconnected. Worse, where would we take two small and confused children for however long it took to fireproof the doors? Gerry left work early and rushed to the solicitor's office, arriving ten minutes before closing time to be told all was well, the work could be done around us as long as we did not use the basement at all. Gerry happily agreed. I'm sure the sellers were furious, but it was their responsibility and should have been done years earlier.

We ate our last meal in Castlewood Drive, reminiscing over the highlights of our first five years of marriage, sorry in many ways to be leaving our friendly neighbours, slightly apprehensive. Last-minute packing and bed-stripping would have to wait until the morning. Celebrating our last night in that bedroom, we neglected to set the alarm, but Suzy never slept beyond 6a.m.
Until the day we moved. Gerry nudged me at 8.
'Someone at the door.'
'Someone' was the driver of the removal van, amazed to see us in dressing gowns, but not as amazed as we were that both children were still asleep.
Panic. How could we dress discreetly with men in brown overalls tramping into all the rooms? There were nappies hanging in the airing cupboard, sheets to strip, kids to feed and dress. I threw on some clothes, picked up the box of eggs I'd kept for breakfast and hustled the children to the neighbour who had offered to look after them.
'Ridiculous to admit, but we all overslept. Would you mind feeding them? Can't stop, loads to do. You're an angel.'
Good neighbours are treasures; there were no raised eyebrows and later in the day we all crammed into her car and followed the furniture van to Vanbrugh Hill. Our rescuer dropped us all off and tactfully, probably with relief, left immediately with her two-year-old.
'Any time,' she said as I thanked her, 'I'll come back in a few days, give you time to unpack.'
As far as I was concerned 'any time' would be centuries away, moving house was far too stressful ever to repeat.

We waved her off and went into a kitchen dominated by a washing machine which took up much of the spare floor space.
We were faced with two major problems. No gas fitter was available until next day, which meant neither hot water nor cooked food; in addition, every ceiling light in the house had bare wires sticking down. Our vendors' removal men had simply cut down the complete fittings. We spent an hour rooting around in packing cases for a couple of table lamps, before attending to rumbling stomachs. We'd heeded advice to carry very little cash with us, credit cards did not yet exist and the banks closed at 3. It was now 3.30 and we were all hungry. We took a bus to Blackheath and chose the cheapest café we could find, not easy in that already upmarket village. Careful study of the menu showed we could

afford fish fingers for the kids and a shared omelette for us. Fortunately we'd unearthed the pushchair and we walked back over the Heath. This pleasant stroll would not normally be a problem, but we were all by now fractious.

On that first night both children shared our bed; we couldn't find sheets for the cot or single bed and the house must have seemed to Sean like a giant's castle. The road outside was the main route to the Blackwall Tunnel (no motorways yet), so the front gate had to be firmly locked. Even if the children found friends in the neighbours' houses there would be no running there unaccompanied, as they had in Eltham. An adult escort would be needed to cross the road, which was totally impossible for anyone in rush hours. The back garden was surrounded by a five-foot brick wall, turning it in a small boy's eyes into a scary fortress.

We'd visited only two or three times and could now examine all the rooms in detail. I loved the curving staircase with its polished mahogany banisters and stained glass windows; the panes of the double doors enclosing the porch were also Victorian stained glass images of birds and flowers. We counted fourteen expensive and newish floral or loudly patterned wallpapers, which we would quickly need to obliterate.
The sitting room, its full-length French windows leading to a narrow conservatory with steps leading down to the well-stocked garden, was fortunately painted in a very soft duck egg blue, except that a huge mirror had been removed, leaving a grubby white space.

The dining room soon became the 'Playroom' because as well as eating, the children spent most of the day playing there, with toys in boxes round the walls. The wallpaper pattern was of lush ivy threaded heavily through a trellis. Gerry often brought me flowers but we could never find them among the paper ivy. This was the first to go!

Can you fall in love with a house? We did. My schoolgirl dream of a big house was fulfilled, I had arrived. But in a fortnight, so would my mother. Peter Pan, Sean's current bedtime book, provided an apt quotation. We' undertaken an awfully big adventure.

AFTERTHOUGHT

I know very little about my parents' early lives, but my family now has a reasonably accurate record of their mother growing up in a time of war and huge social change.

In editing these pages I have noticed several themes, which were not deliberate. First the overwhelming influence of school and an emphasis on being clever that seems at times like showing off. It is perhaps myself I need to convince.

Then there is my inability to stand up to a mother who was herself a very sad person. Her father's suicide, her brother's jealousy, her own unacknowledged intelligence contaminated her adult life. Have I inherited her silent anger? Yes, plus possibly some of her manipulative ways, but not her obsession with housework. I would never live with any of my children and in fear of being too possessive I may have overdone my eagerness for them to leave home.

I regret my shameful dismissal of my father. Social mobility can create havoc in family life and he too had his demons. I absorbed the 'not good enough' mantra and am too quick to imagine rejection, but had he lived we might have become closer through his grandson. My parents' demands that I do well at school gave me a thirst for achievement and as a working mother in the thirties Mum offered a strong role model.

Above all, a sense of humour is a great survival tool.

ACKNOWLEDGEMENTS

Impossible to name everyone who has encouraged me, offered practical help or jogged my memory, but here are a few specific thanks

Books:
Simon Garfield: Our Hidden Lives, Diaries of post-war Britain
(Ebury Press 2004)
David Kynaston: Austerity Britain 1945 -51; Family Britain 1951 – 57
(Bloomsbury 2007/9)
Mary Stott (Editor): Women Talking, An anthology from The Guardian Women's Page.   (Pandora Press 1987)

Computer support: Dave McCaighy for patience way beyond the call of duty in teaching me new Word tricks, then teaching me again. My children - Robyn, for cover design and hours spent with Photoshop; Sean, who was impressed by my creating a blog, advised on some of its content and shared it on Facebook; Suzy, for added assistance to an ageing Mum who is less computer-literate than she pretends.

Feedback Group: Rebecca Milligan, Boris Rumney, Tom Thompson, Alan Wallace and Greg Watts for their invaluable and constructive comments.

Proofreading: David Firth for his impeccable accuracy. Any possible errors remaining will have resulted from my last-minute additions.

Stamford High School
Rachel Petrie and Adam Cox for help via SHS archives.
Barbara Midgley, former Head of Classics after my time, for on-line news of former friends.
SHS School Magazines 1946 – 1950 (my own copies)

Special mention
Robyn, my youngest, for her generosity over the fact that she is not mentioned. She says it only confirms her suspicion that she was in fact adopted, although she was not born for another couple of years.

BLOG: https://gettingitdownonpaper.wordpress.com/

Lightning Source UK Ltd.
Milton Keynes UK
UKHW011948071019

351169UK00002B/167/P

9 781786 101693